THE TIMECHART HISTORY OF

REVOLUTIONS

THE TIMECHART HISTORY OF

REVOLUTIONS

PASCAL THIVILLON

NICOLA CHALTON

MEREDITH MACARDLE

WORTH
PRESS

First published in 2007 by Worth Press Ltd
www.worthpress.co.uk

© Worth Press Ltd, concept, editorial, design, layout and panel sequence, 2007

This book was created by Basement Press, London
www.basementpress.com
Original concept, design and layout
Editorial
Cartography

British Library Cataloguing in Publication Data
A catalogue record for this book is available from the British Library

ISBN-10: 1-903025-38-9
ISBN-13: 978-1-903025-38-3

Printed and bound in Thailand

10 9 8 7 6 5 4 3 2 1

The publisher wishes to thank the following institutions for the use of illustrations in this book: **Heritage Image Partnership** cover (Ann Ronan Picture Library);
page 10: bottom left (Ann Ronan Picture Library); page 22: top left (Ann Ronan Picture Library); center right (Ann Ronan Picture Library); page 28: bottom right (Art Media);
page 32: top right (Museum of London); page 40: top right (Art Media), page 42: center left (Art Media – Carnavalet, Paris), page 43: bottom right (Art Media); page 48
top right (Art Media); page 59: center left (Ann Ronan Picture Library); page 60: top right (Ann Ronan Picture Library); page 62: center left (Art Media – Gallery Tretyakov,
Moscow); page 68: top right (Art Media); page 72: top right (Ann Ronan Picture Library). **Rex Features** page 56: top right (Haber); page 57: top right; page 58: bottom
right (Pacific Press Service); page 59: top right (Pacific Press Service), bottom right; page 64: top right (Sipa Press); page 65: bottom right (Sipa Press); page 66: top right
(photo Enrique Meneses); page 69: top right (Sipa Press); page 70: top right (Sipa Press); page 71: top right (photo Simon Townsley). **Visipix.com** page 2; page 9: second
row left, third row right; page 10: top right, center left, center right; page 11: second row right, third row right; page 12: first row right, third row center; page 13: bottom
left; page 14: fourth row right, fourth row left; page 16: double-barreled gun, center right, bottom left; page 17: third row right (photo Juerg Derrer), page 20: first row,
second row; page 34: top right, Philip II, William I of Orange; page 35: top right; page 43: center left; page 44: top right; page 45: bottom right. **Library of Congress**
page 9: second row right, third row right, fourth row left; page 11: fourth row left; page 12: third row right, fourth row left; page 13: top left, center; bottom right; page
14: first row left, second row right; page 15: first row left, third row left; page 16: colt .45; bottom left; page 17: first row left, first row right, second row left, second row
right, third row center; page 18: second row, third row, fourth row; page 19: center left, center right, bottom left; page 20: third row center, third row right; page 21: first
row left, second row left, second row center; page 22: bottom right, bottom left; page 23: second row left, second row right; page 24: first row right; second row, third
row; page 25: top right, bottom left; page 29: third row; page 35: King Charles I; page 36: top left, top right, King George III, George Washington; page 37: bottom left,
Paul Revere; page 38: top right, bottom left, bottom right; page 39: bottom left; page 40: Maximilien Robespierre, Georges Danton, Jean-Paul Marat, Honoré Riqueti; page
41: top left, bottom left, King Louis XVI; page 42: bottom left; page 45: center right, Miguel Hidalgo; page 46: top right; page 47: top right, Giuseppe Garibaldi, Lajos
Kossuth; page 48: bottom right, Sitting Bull, Red Cloud, Spotted Elk; page 49: top right, center right, George A. Custer, Nelson A. Miles; page 50: top right, Abraham
Lincoln, David Glasgow Farragut, Ulysses Simpson Grant, George Brinton McClellan, Jefferson Davis, Thomas Jonathan Jackson, Robert Edward Lee; page 51: top right,
bottom right, bottom right; page 52: top left, top right; page 53: center left, center right, Sir Claude Maxwell MacDonald; page 54: top left, top right, Porfirio Díaz, Victoriano
Huerta, Francisco I. Madero; page 55: top right, center left, Pancho Villa; page 57: Chiang Kai-shek; page 58: top right; page 60: Vladimir Lenin, Joseph Stalin, Alexander
Kerensky; page 62: Karl Marx; page 63: top left; page 66: Fidel Castro; page 67: top right. **National Archives and Records Administration** page 20: third row left; page
24: first row left; page 25: center; page 26: second row left, second row right; page 27: second row left; page 29: second row left (photo Cecil Stoughton), fourth row left
(photo Jack E. Kightlinger); page 30: first row left; page 39: top right, bottom right; page 49: bottom right; page 57: Deng Xiaoping; page 67: center right, bottom right.
US Department of Defence page 29: second row right; page 30: fourth row left, fourth row right; page 31: bottom right. **National Aeronautics and Space
Administration** page 31: top right, bottom left. **European Communities, 1995–2005** page 29: fifth row. **Cyber Media Services** other portraits not already listed and
not in public domain.

Publisher's Note Every effort has been made to ensure the accuracy of the information presented in this book. The publisher will not assume liability for damages caused
by inaccuracies in the data and makes no warranty whatsoever expressed or implied. The publisher welcomes comments and corrections from readers, emailed to
worthpress@aol.com, which will be considered for incorporation in future editions. Likewise, every effort has been made to trace copyright holders and seek permission to
use illustrative and other material. The publisher wishes to apologize for any inadvertent errors or omissions and would be glad to rectify these in future editions.

Contents

World Map
showing locations of major revolutions and civil wars through history   6–7

Timechart of Revolutions, Civil Wars, and Rebellions

1190 BCE–1210 CE	9
1211–1710	11–12
1711–1760	14–15
1761–1810	17–18
1811–1860	20–21
1861–1910	23–24
1911–1960	26–27
1961–Present	29–30

Fold-out Flaps

Armies of the Ancient World	10
Japanese Samurai	13
Weaponry	16
The Role of the Church	19
The Industrial Revolution	22
Ideologies and Propaganda	25
Colonial Wars of Independence	28
Terrorism	31

Featured Conflicts

Revolts against Rome	32
Early Peasant Revolts in China	33
The Dutch Revolt	34
The English Civil Wars	35
The American Revolution	36–39
The French Revolution	40–43
The Latin American Revolutions	44–45
The Zulu Civil Wars	46
1848 Revolutions	47
The Native American Revolts	48–49
The American Civil War	50–51
The Boxer Rebellion	52–53
The Mexican Revolution	54–55
The Chinese Revolution	56–59
The Russian Revolution	60–63
The Spanish Civil War	64–65
The Cuban Revolution	66–67
The Algerian War of Independence	68
The Cambodian Civil War	69
The Iranian Revolution	70
The Balkans Conflict	71
The Bloodless Revolutionaries	72

World Map

Human history is one of almost continuous warfare, including many wars to do with who did the ruling, and how they ruled. Most early revolutionaries simply wanted to replace a bad ruler with a better one, or were fighting for national independence. Only much later did revolutionaries begin to fight because of ideological theories about ideal states. This book traces the steps of all these rebels, from the ancient world to today's terrorists, taking in peasant revolts, religious wars, idealism, and power-mad dictators. In more than 3,000 years of history, the major revolutions and civil wars are:

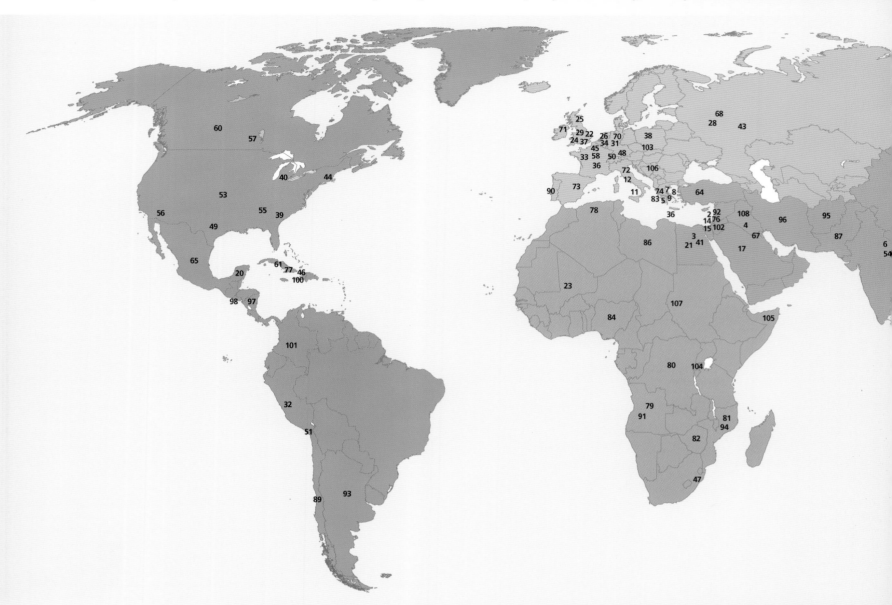

1   Zhou uprising, China, c. 1040 BCE
2   Israelite civil wars, c. 1000 and 922 BCE
3   Egyptians overthrow Assyrian rule, 664–10 BCE
4   Civil war in Babylonia, c. 627 BCE
5   Messenian revolt against Spartan rule, 650 BCE
6   Struggles for supremacy in the Ganges Valley, India, c. 600 BCE
7   Greek revolts against Persian control, 495–48 BCE
8   Revolts against Spartan or Athenian control in Peloponnesian Wars, 457–03 BCE
9   Democratic revolt in Athens against oligarchic Council of Four, 411 BCE
10 Mauryan rebellion, India, 321 BCE
11 Servile Wars (slave uprisings against Rome), 135–32 BCE, 104–03 BCE, 73–71 BCE
12 Roman civil wars, 49–45 BCE, 8–35 BCE, 43–42 BCE, 32–31 BCE
13 Trung sisters Vietnamese rebellion, c. 40–43 CE
14 Jewish Zealot rebellion in Jerusalem and Masada against Rome, 66–73 CE
15 Bar Kochba Jewish revolt against Rome, 132–35
16 "Yellow Turbans" peasant uprising, China, 184–205
17 First Muslim civil war, Arabia, 656–661
18 Huang Chao's uprising, China, 870s–81
19 Gempei wars, Japan, 1180–85
20 Mayan civil war, 1200

21 Mameluke uprising, Egypt, 1250
22 Barons' revolt, England, 1215
23 Sundiata's rebellion against the Sosso Empire, Mali, 1235
24 Llewellyn ap Gruffydd's Welsh rebellion against England, 1256–83
25 Scotland's war of independence from England, 1296–1346
26 Peasants' revolt, Flanders, 1323–28
27 "Red Turbans" revolt, China, 1350s–68
28 Great feudal war, Russia, 1425–53
29 Wars of the Roses, England/Wales, 1455–87
30 Warring States period, Japan, 1467–1615
31 Peasants' war, Germany, 1524–25
32 Inca succession struggle, 1527–32
33 French wars of religion, 1562–98
34 Dutch war of independence, 1568–1648
35 Thailand's war of independence from Burma, 1584
36 Fronde civil wars, France, 1649, 1650–52
37 English civil wars, 1642–60
38 Bohdan Chmielnicki's Cossack rebellion, Poland, 1648
39 Stono slave rebellion, America, 1739
40 Pontiac's war, America, 1763–64
41 Mameluke revolt, Egypt, 1768
42 Tay Son rebellion, Vietnam, 1771–88
43 Pugachev's rebellion, Russia, 1773–74

THE AGE OF REVOLUTION, c. 1750–1800

44 American revolution, 1775–83

The first revolution in "The Age of Revolution", and therefore deeply influential. The war was fought for the principle of liberty, and proved that:
1 - Ordinary citizens can overthrow despotic or misrepresentative governments.
2 - Ideals of liberty can be acted upon and bring about change.
  American revolutionaries were concerned with rights, but were aiming at political, not social revolution. There was no real attempt to improve social conditions, so it did not have the lasting and world-wide impact of the French Revolution. Instead, it was most influential on its near neighbors, giving partial inspiration to the slave revolt in Haiti and, in particular, the Latin American revolutions against Spain. Apart from in Mexico, these too were not social revolutions, but were led by colonial elites who wanted to take up the reins of government, not overthrow social order.

45 French revolution, 1789

The roots of most future revolutions, and certainly revolutionary theory, lay in the French Revolution, which was concerned with social problems as much as with political liberty. It threw up the first questions of class and class conflict, questions which have occupied revolutionaries such as Blanqui, Marx, Engels, Lenin, Trotsky, and others ever since.
  French revolutionaries were determined to throw off every last vestige of the *ancien régime* – whereas earlier revolutions had usually adopted similar institutions to the ones overthrown – and, for the first time, proposed the idea that revolutionary change was social progress. Although it paved the way for political parties and theorists on the left, it also sparked the development of conservative, right-wing factions dedicated to defending a traditional or established order. So, it even influenced right-wing revolutions such as the revolt by Spanish army officers precipitating the Spanish Civil War.
  France also took the lead in later revolutions, particularly the upheavals in Europe in 1830 and in 1848.

46 Haitian uprising, 1791–1804

Inspired by the examples of America and France, Haitian slaves rose up in the only slave revolt which was successful enough to take over a European colony.

70	German revolution, 1918	**74**	Greek civil war, 1945–49
71	Irish war of independence, 1920–21, and civil war, 1922–23	**75**	First Indochina War/Vietnamese war of independence, 1946–54
72	Fascist revolution, Italy, 1922	**76**	Israeli war of independence, 1948–49
73	Spanish civil war, 1936–39		

77 Cuban revolution, 1953–59

Although aiming at idealistic socialist hopes of political freedom and social improvements, the imperative for the Cuban Revolution came not from the working classes, but from intellectuals and revolutionary theorists. Only later did the new regime formally identify itself with the communist world. This revolution saw the creation of a revolutionary icon, Che Guevara, whose beliefs in the necessity for armed uprising inspired guerrilla movements and left-wingers around the world.

78	Algerian war of independence, 1954–62	**93**	Military coup, Argentina, 1976
79	Angolan war of independence, 1961–75	**94**	Mozambique civil war, 1976–94
80	Mobutu's coup d'etat, Congo (Zaire), 1965	**95**	Afghanistan civil wars/Russian invasion, 1978–89
81	Mozambique war of independence, 1965–75	**96**	Iranian revolution, 1979
82	Rhodesia (Zimbabwe), war of independence/civil war, 1965–79	**97**	Nicaraguan revolution, 1979
83	Greek "Colonels" coup, Apr 21, 1967	**98**	El Salvadorean civil war, 1979–92
84	Nigeria/Biafra civil war, 1967–70	**99**	Tamil Tiger insurrection, Sri Lanka, 1983–
85	Cambodian civil war, 1968–75	**100**	Haitian revolution, 1985–86
86	Gaddafi's coup, Libya, Sep 1, 1969	**101**	Colombian civil war, 1986–
87	Pakistan civil war and breakaway of Bangladesh, 1971	**102**	Palestinian "intifada" uprising, Israel, 1987
88	Philippines Moro insurrection, 1971–96	**103**	East European anti-communist "revolutions", 1989
89	Military coup, Chile, 1973	**104**	Rwandan civil war/Hutu genocide of Tutsis, 1990–94
90	Revolution of the Flowers, Portugal, 1974	**105**	Somalian civil war, 1991–95
91	Angolan civil wars, 1975–92	**106**	Yugoslav civil wars, 1991–2001
92	Lebanese civil war, 1975–90	**107**	Arab Sudan ethnic cleansing of Darfur, 2003–
		108	Sectarian violence in Iraq, 2006
		109	Military coup, Thailand, 2006

African civil wars since independence

Caused by poverty, failure of corrupt or incompetent political institutions, competition over natural resources, ethnic and religious tensions, there have been civil wars in nearly half the African countries south of the Sahara in the last 20 years. It is now the region with the greatest number of conflicts. About one-fifth of the African population lives in a country which is either formally at war or in which a low-intensity conflict is continuing. In many cases, the rebels are concerned not with gaining justice or political power, but with winning control of "loot" such as diamond fields.

Latin American civil wars

Fierce ideological differences between socialists/communists and right-wing groups were complicated by America's interference to protect its interests and to oppose communism. Death squads, disappearances, and military dictatorships were commonplace, sparking guerrilla wars in opposition. Many Latin American countries, e.g. Colombia, are still divided with regular armed conflict. Others, e.g. Peru and Mexico, contend with guerrilla groups, often ethnically based. Since World War II the most common cause for a change in government in Latin America has not been elections, but a coup d'etat.

There are at least ten country leaders today who came to power through a military coup. They include Colonel Gaddafi in Libya (1969), General Musharraf in Pakistan (1999–), and Sonthi Boonyaratglin in Thailand (2006).

Internal civil war is now the most predominant form of military conflict.

47	First Zulu civil wars, 1817–19	**57**	Red River rebellion, Canada, 1869–70
48	Revolutions in Europe (France, Germany, Belgium, Italy, Poland), 1830	**58**	Paris Commune, France, 1871
		59	Satsuma rebellion, Japan, 1877
49	Texan revolution, 1835–36	**60**	North-West rebellion, Canada, 1885
50	"Year of Revolutions", Europe, 1848	**61**	Cuban revolution, 1895–98
51	Latin American revolutions, 1810–26	**62**	Philippines war of independence, 1896–99
52	Taiping rebellion, China, 1850–64		
53	Plains Native American revolts, 1854–90	**63**	Boxer rebellion, China, 1899–1901
		64	"Young Turks" revolution, Turkey, 1908
54	Indian mutiny, 1857–58	**65**	Mexican revolution, 1910–20
55	American civil war, 1861–65	**66**	Chinese revolution, 1911
56	Apache wars, USA, 1863–86	**67**	Arab revolt, 1916

68 Russian revolution and civil war, 1917–21

Building on socialist theories that had developed following the French Revolution, particularly on Marx's analysis of history and revolution, the Russian communist revolution began with idealistic ideas of improving society for all its members, and degenerated into state-run terror.

The Soviet Union had an enormous effect on world politics in the 20th century, fomenting other communist take-overs in eastern Europe, and funding communist parties around the world, especially in China. The "Cold War" between communist and American-supported ideologies added to the possibility of violent regime changes.

69 Chinese civil war, 1927–49

Splitting from its former mentor and partner, the USSR, in the 1960s, Chinese communism took its own direction under Chairman Mao.

The influence on peasant-based revolutionary groups around the world was enormous, and, like the USSR, China played a part in supporting revolutions in many other countries, particularly the major wars in Asia: the Korean War, the Vietnam War, and the Cambodian civil war.

The Timeline History of Revolutions, Civil Wars, and Rebellions

This Timeline presents a chronological overview of the world's great revolutions, civil wars, and rebellions, along with many smaller uprisings, insurrections, and movements that led to social, political, and economic change. Key events in World history are also included.

The Timeline is divided into five geographical regions:

EUROPE

AMERICAS

AFRICA

MIDDLE EAST & ASIA*

AUSTRALIA & OCEANIA

Following events vertically on the Timeline shows what was happening in different parts of the world at any one point in time, and illustrates the spread of revolution and rebellion from region to region.

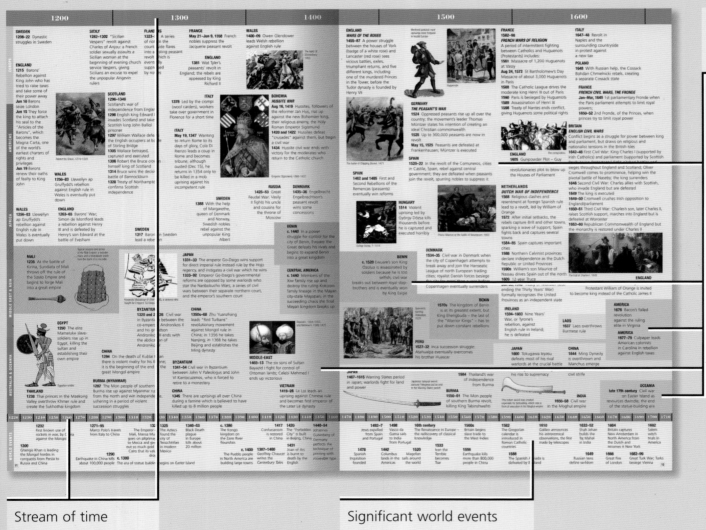

Horizontal flow-lines divide the chart into geographical areas

Stream of time

Significant world events

Fold-out flaps offer close-up views of subjects related to the Timeline.

More detailed examinations of a selection of revolutions and other conflicts are covered on the pages that follow the Timeline (pages 32–72).

* including Egypt, reflecting its links with Syria and Palestine

Early Peasant Revolts in China

Many Chinese dynasties fell because of rebellions. In some cases these uprisings were led not by generals or noblemen, but by the ordinary people, the peasants. A vast country with a predominantly rural population, China has always had thousands – if not millions – of peasants. Poor, often mistreated, seldom owning the land they worked, and at the mercy of poor weather which could cause famine and starvation, they had nothing to lose in a war, and were often driven to armed revolt against the landlords and nobles. Most of their rebellions were suppressed. But, if they grouped in large enough numbers and found a strong leader, these humble farmers found they could have a devastating effect on China.

Illustration from *The Romance of the Three Kingdoms*, a Chinese historical novel written by Luo Guanzhyng in the 14th century; the Yellow Turbans revolt is the opening event of the book

CAUSES

Any event which upset the peasants' fragile economic stability: high taxes; poor crops; feudal burdens; abuse by landlords; civil wars. Peasants were also easily influenced by revolutionary ideals.

CONSEQUENCES

Most revolts were put down by local nobles or by imperial forces. However, some rebellions contributed to the break-up of the state, or even directly toppled ruling dynasties.

KEY REVOLTS

184–205 Yellow Turbans' Revolt against Han dynasty (206 BCE–220 CE). With high taxes and widespread corruption causing unrest, peasants in north China adopt the beliefs of a Taoist sect, led by Zhang Jiao and his brothers, that all people are equal and land should be distributed equally. Zhang leads them in an uprising, aiming to capture the capital, Luoyang. Rebels identify themselves by wearing yellow headdresses or scarves. When Zhang dies from illness in 188 the rebels lose momentum, but they are only defeated when landlords unite together. These new warlords then begin to reject the authority of the weakened Han dynasty. The country soon crumbles into civil wars of the bloody Three Kingdoms period (220–280).

875–84 Huang Chao's Rebellion against Tang dynasty (618–907). Together with Wang Xianzhi, who started the revolt in 874, Huang Chao leads overtaxed peasants in a massive uprising in Henan and Shandong provinces. At one point he has 600,000 followers. The rebels soon control vast areas in the east. In 879 Huang captures Guangzhou and kills most of the 200,000 population. In 881 Huang takes the capital Xi'an (Chang'an), putting the emperor to flight. Huang then declares himself emperor of a new Qi dynasty. But, the Tang government regroups, and in 884 defeats the rebels. Huang flees and commits suicide. The rebellion weakens the government so much that when the successful generals start to take political powers, the Tang dynasty collapses.

1350s–68 Red Turbans' Revolt against Yuan dynasty (1271–1368). Rebels identify themselves by wearing red headdresses or scarves. In 1352 the former peasant and Buddhist monk Zhu Yuanzhang (Chu Yuan-chang) joins one of the peasant groups and begins to rise to prominence. He proves to be an excellent general when fighting breaks out soon afterwards. In 1356 Zhu captures Nanjing. He goes on to soundly defeat the Yuan, taking their capital of Beijing (Peking). In 1368 Zhu declares the Yuan are defeated, and founds a new dynasty, the Ming. According to legend, fortune cookies originate from the Red Turban practice of passing messages hidden inside cakes. A major campaign organized with the words "Rise up on the 15th of the 8th moon" lies behind the tradition of festival mooncakes.

KEY PERSONALITIES

Zhang Jiao (Zhang Jue), 140–188
"Popular" Taoist, offering mainly charms and potions rather than philosophy. Promotes idealistic theories which are adopted by peasants. **184** Leads his followers in Yellow Turbans' armed uprising. Calls himself "Great Teacher".

Huang Chao, ?–884
A salt smuggler from Shandong province. **875** Joins Wang Xianzhi's peasant rebellion. Becomes known as main leader of the revolt. Calls himself the "Heaven-Storming General". **881** Declares himself emperor, but gains no support outside his armies. **884** Kills himself when it is clear he is defeated.

Zhu Yuanzhang (Chu Yuan-chang), 1328–98
The founder of the Ming dynasty of Imperial China, considered to be one of the greatest emperors; born in a poor peasant family in Anhui province. **c. 1346** His parents die of starvation; he has no option other than to enter a Buddhist monastery; learns to read and write. **1352** Joins one of the peasant Red Turban groups, rebelling against the unpopular Mongol or Yuan dynasty. Becomes dominant rebel leader; meets and learns from rebel scholars. **1368** Overthrows the Mongols, and proclaims himself emperor. The name he chooses for his reign, Hongwu (Hung-wu), means "Immensely Martial". Introduces important legal and social reforms, including measures to help peasants and small farmers.

The Dutch Revolt, or Eighty Years' War

The battle of Gibraltar (fighting did not take place only in the Netherlands): on April 25, 1607 a Dutch fleet surprised and engaged a Spanish fleet anchored at the Bay of Gibraltar; during the 4-hour action, the entire Spanish fleet was destroyed

In 1568 the Netherlands, or Low Countries, were part of the vast Spanish Empire. A collection of states and independent towns, the seven northern provinces were mainly Calvinist (Friesland, Gelderland, Groningen, Holland, Overijssel, Utrecht, and Zeeland), whereas the ten southern provinces were Catholic (Antwerp, Artois, Brabant, Flanders, Limburg, Luxembourg, Hainaut, Mechlin, Namur, and Zutphen). Following the revolt, the northern provinces became an independent republic called the United Provinces or the Netherlands, although many foreign countries began to call it by the name of its wealthiest and most important state, Holland. The southern provinces were now called the Spanish Netherlands. Much later on these divided into modern Belgium and Luxembourg, or became parts of France and Germany.

The Low Countries after the Peace of Munster (1648)

The Dutch Republic

Spanish provinces

GRONINGEN
Groningen
Leeuwarden
FRIESLAND
(DRENTHE)
Zwolle
NORTH SEA
Amsterdam
HOLLAND
OVERIJSSEL
UTRECHT
Zutphen
Utrecht
Rotterdam
GELDERLAND
ZEELAND
's-Hertogenbosch
Middelburg
NORTH BRABANT
Bruges
Antwerp
HOLY ROMAN EMPIRE
FLANDERS
BRABANT
PRINCIPALITY OF LIÈGE
Brussels
Maastricht
Liège
LIMBURG
ARTOIS
NAMUR
Arras
HAINAUT
LUXEMBOURG
FRANCE
Luxembourg

CAUSES

Resentment at Foreign Rule The Spanish king, Philip II, was not interested in the Netherlands. He was unpopular and the Spanish officials he put in place were deeply resented. The Dutch nobles complained that the country was being run by foreigners.

Religious Clashes Calvinism, a form of Protestantism, had spread widely in the Netherlands. Philip, however, was devoutly Catholic. He introduced the dreaded Spanish Inquisition to try to stop what he saw as heresy.

Power Struggles Philip was an absolutist monarch – he believed that, as king, he and he alone should have the power to make laws. He also wanted to impose centralized government in his empire. But the Dutch states and towns thought they should have some autonomy and authority.

High Taxes With a long-standing merchant tradition, the Netherlands had become a wealthy part of the Spanish Empire. The Dutch resented seeing that wealth creamed off in tax money to support King Philip's wars.

CONSEQUENCES

• The Netherlands divided into two. The seven northern provinces became an independent republic.

• English support for the rebels led to war between Spain and England. In 1588 Spain sent the Armada, a massive fleet, to invade England. It was destroyed. This, and defeats by the rebel navy (known as the Sea Beggars), meant that Spain lost its position as the dominant European sea power.

• The new nation took on a distinct character when its parliament passed several reforms including a Bill of Rights and the right to a free press. Prosperous and tolerant, the United Provinces became a center for freethinkers, philosophers, and artists.

• Formerly rich cities in the south such as Bruges, Antwerp, Ghent, and Brussels became less important. Cities in the north – Amsterdam, The Hague, and Rotterdam – began to develop as trading centers.

• Dutch sea power and global trading links, particularly with the Far East, made the nation important within Europe.

SPANISH LEADERS

Philip II, King of Spain, 1527–98
Brought up to consider himself an absolute ruler, convinced of his own righteousness. Devout Catholic, thought of himself as champion of the church. Bankrupted Spain through continuous warfare. **1556** Becomes king of Spain and of the Netherlands. **1590 and 1591** Sends his armies from the Netherlands to help French Catholics, allowing the Dutch to regroup.

Fernando Álvarez de Toledo, 3rd Duke of Alba (Alva), 1507–82
General, governor of the Spanish Netherlands from 1567 to 1573. Nicknamed "the Iron Duke" because of his repressive policies. **1567** Opens hated "Council of Blood", a tribunal which executes thousands for heresy or treason. Imposes an unpopular new sales tax. **1568** Responds harshly to revolt, allowing his soldiers to sack captured cities.

Alessandro Farnese, Duke of Parma, 1545–92
General, diplomat, statesman. **1578** Becomes governor of the Netherlands. **1579** Entices the Catholic "Malcontent" nobles of the southern provinces back to Spanish allegiance. **1589** Restores Spanish authority in all parts of the south.

DUTCH REVOLUTIONARIES

William I of Orange, the Silent, 1533–84
First leader, and financier, of the revolt. Known as "the Silent" because he disliked talking about controversial issues. Also known as "Father of the Fatherland": Dutch national anthem, "The Wilhelmus", was written in his honor and Dutch flag was based on his own. **1568** Inspires initial opposition to Spain. **1584** Assassinated.

Maurice of Nassau, 1567–1625
William's son. Talented, innovative military leader. Studied warfare as a science. **1588** Appointed to lead Dutch army and navy. Becomes expert in siege warfare, successfully conducts Dutch strategy of besieging or relieving cities, and conducting guerrilla warfare. **1609** Bitterly opposes truce. **1621** On renewed outbreak of war cannot match his previous successes.

Piet Pieterszoon Heyn (Hein), 1577–1629
Admiral, Sea Beggar, folk hero. **1623** Raids Spanish ships and ports in the West Indies as a privateer (authorized pirate). **May 20, 1628** Captures entire Spanish treasure fleet off Cuba. **1629** Blockades Spanish privateers based in Belgian city of Duinkerken. Killed in action.

THE ARTICLES OF CONFEDERATION

For several years, the newly declared independent states of America were governed not by British law or by the American Constitution, but by the Articles of Confederation. Agreed to by the Third Continental Congress on November 15, 1777, ratified and in force from March 1, 1781, the Articles were only replaced by the Constitution when it was ratified by New Hampshire on June 21, 1788. The Articles formally declared that the colonies were now independent states, "the United States of America".

Contents of the Articles of Confederation

Preamble
Article I – Name of Confederation
Article II – States' Rights
Article III – Mutual defense
Article IV – Freedom of movement; extradition
Article V – Defines Congress
Article VI – Restrictions on states' rights
Article VII – Appointment of military officers
Article VIII – Taxes
Article IX – Congress's powers
Article X – Committee of States
Article XI – Canada and other states may join the United States
Article XII – Payment of debt
Article XIII – Authority of Congress; Union is perpetual; amendments
Conclusion
Signatories

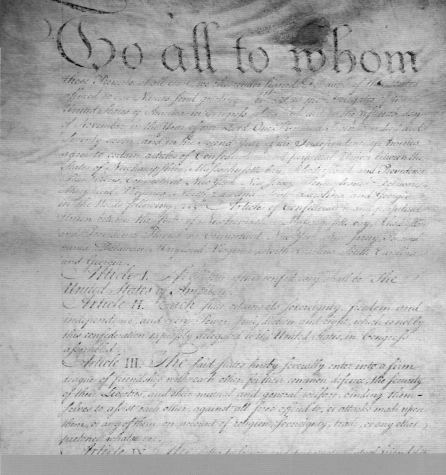

EXTRACT FROM THE ARTICLES OF CONFEDERATION

Preamble To all to whom these Presents shall come, we the undersigned Delegates of the States affixed to our Names send greeting.
Articles of Confederation and perpetual Union between the States of New Hampshire, Massachusetts bay, Rhode Island and Providence Plantations, Connecticut, New York, New Jersey, Pennsylvania, Delaware, Maryland, Virginia, North Carolina, South Carolina and Georgia.

Article I The Stile of this Confederacy shall be "The United States of America."

Article II Each state retains its sovereignty, freedom, and independence, and every power, jurisdiction, and right, which is not by this Confederation expressly delegated to the United States, in Congress assembled.

Article III The said States hereby severally enter into a firm league of friendship with each other, for their common defense, the security of their liberties, and their mutual and general welfare, binding themselves to assist each other, against all force offered to, or attacks made upon them, or any of them, on account of religion, sovereignty, trade, or any other pretense whatever.

Article IV The better to secure and perpetuate mutual friendship and intercourse among the people of the different States in this Union, the free inhabitants of each of these States, paupers, vagabonds, and fugitives from justice excepted, shall be entitled to all privileges and immunities of free citizens in the several States; and the people of each State shall free ingress and regress to and from any other State, and shall enjoy therein all the privileges of trade and commerce, subject to the same duties, impositions . . .

The Articles and the Constitution contain much material in common, but by the time of the Constitution the "Founding Fathers" decided upon some changes. These gave more powers to central government. The changes include:

Legislature
Articles: Congress, one house
Constitution: Congress, divided into two houses: the House of Representatives and the Senate

Chair of Legislature
Articles: President of Congress
Constitution: Speaker of the House of Representatives

Executive Branch
Articles: None
Constitution: President heads an executive branch

Taxes Raised By
Articles: The states
Constitution: Congress

National Courts
Articles: None
Constitution: Federal courts and the Supreme Court

Relationship Between States
Articles: A "league of friendship" of sovereign states
Constitution: Political union with Constitution as supreme law

Disputes Between States
Articles: Settled by Congress
Constitution: Settled by Supreme Court

Trade Between States
Articles: No regulations
Constitution: Regulated by Congress

EXTRACT FROM THE DECLARATION OF INDEPENDENCE

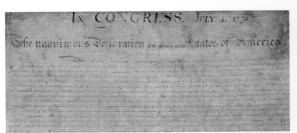

In Congress, July 4, 1776
The unanimous Declaration of the thirteen united States of America

When in the Course of human events, it becomes necessary for one people to dissolve the political bands which have connected them with another, and to assume among the powers of the earth, the separate and equal station to which the Laws of Nature and of Nature's God entitle them, a decent respect to the opinions of mankind requires that they should declare the causes which impel them to the separation. We hold these truths to be self-evident, that all men are created equal, that they are endowed by their Creator with certain unalienable Rights, that among these are Life, Liberty and the pursuit of Happiness. -- That to secure these rights, Governments are instituted among Men, deriving their just Powers from the consent of the governed, -- That whenever any Form of Government becomes destructive of these ends, it is the Right of the People to alter or to abolish it, and to institute new Government, laying its foundation on such principles and organizing its powers in such form, as to them shall seem most likely to effect their Safety and Happiness. Prudence, indeed, will dictate that Governments long established should not be changed for light and transient causes; and accordingly all experience hath shewn, that mankind are more disposed to suffer, while evils are sufferable, than to right themselves by abolishing the forms to which they are accustomed. But when a long train of abuses and usurpations, pursuing invariably the same Object evinces a design to reduce them under absolute Despotism, it is their right, it is their duty, to throw off such Government, and to provide new Guards . . .

(Left to right): Benjamin Franklin, John Adams, and Thomas Jefferson reviewing a draft of the Declaration of Independence

The French Revolution

The French Revolution, a victory for republicanism and democracy over absolute monarchy, came to influence events across the world. King Louis XVI of France faced simultaneous challenges from members of the elite, the population of Paris, and the rural poor. He was unable to control the situation, and violence erupted in 1789. The storming of the Bastille in Paris, on 14 July of that year, was the symbolic end to the *ancien régime*.

On the morning of July 14, 1789, a crowd advanced on the Bastille, the state prison in Paris, to ask the governor to release the prisoners (there were only seven) and weapons in the building; the governor was evasive and the people stormed the fortress

CAUSES

Absolute Government of the King During the 17th and 18th centuries, France was ruled by kings who controlled all political power. As the ideals of the Enlightenment began to spread, the French people resented the power that King Louis XVI had over them. The king seemed more interested in hunting than governing France, and with his Austrian queen, Marie Antoinette, his extravagant lifestyle seemed at odds with the harsh conditions most other people had to endure.

Inefficient and Unjust Government The government was inefficient, unjust, and corrupt. The French parliament ("Estates-General"), made up of the 1st Estate clergy, the 2nd Estate nobility, and the 3rd Estate commoners, had not met since 1614 and could only meet with the consent of the king. The tax system and the privileges of the clergy and nobility were unjust.

Financial and Social Difficulties France had been at war regularly during the last 100 years, including in support of the American Revolution. The country was bankrupt and unemployment and bread prices were high. Louis XVI's attempts to reform the tax system to raise money were blocked by the nobility and clergy.

CONSEQUENCES

• Collapse of France's *ancien régime* (the old system based on the Three Estates), including feudalism and the privileges of the clergy and nobility.

• Creation of a new establishment based on the "Declaration of the Rights of Man", one of the most far-reaching documents of the world.

• Social and economic reform in France, including abolition of slavery.

• Spread of ideas of nationalism and democracy: the French democratic slogan "Liberty, Equality, Fraternity" was adopted by oppressed peoples around the world.

• Introduction of the idea of limited monarchy.

Cost of the Revolution The Reign of Terror (1793–94), in which nobles, clergy, and anyone who posed a threat to the revolution were executed, caused social and political instability that took years to overcome and made the dictatorship of Napoleon inevitable. Around 17,000 people were executed under the revolutionary laws, and many more were massacred without trial. Hundreds of thousands were arrested and imprisoned, many of whom died in captivity.

RADICALS

Maximilien Robespierre, 1758–94
Lawyer, a leader of the Jacobin Club (radical revolutionaries), and member of the Commitee of Public Safety ruling France during the revolution. **May 1789** Elected to Estates-General. **1791** Appointed Public Accuser. **1792** Forms Revolutionary Tribunal. **1793–94** Instrumental in Reign of Terror. **Jul 1794** Denounced, tried, and executed.

Georges Danton, 1759–94
Lawyer and president of the Cordeliers Club (radical revolutionary party). **Aug 1792** Appointed Minister of Justice. **May 1793** Leader in purge of Girondists (moderates) from National Convention. **Apr 1793** Joins Committee of Public Safety. Unlike Robespierre he is opposed to excesses of Reign of Terror. **Apr 1794** Tried and executed after Robespierre denounces him as a counter-revolutionary.

Jean-Paul Marat, 1743–93
Physician and editor of revolutionary newspaper *L'ami du Peuple* ("The Friend of the People"). **Sep 1792** Advocates September Massacres (murder of political prisoners). **Sep 1792** Elected to National Convention. **May 1793** Campaigns against Girondists. **Jul 1793** Stabbed to death in his bathtub by Charlotte Corday, a Girondist activist.

MODERATES

Honoré Riqueti, Comte de Mirabeau, 1749–91
Soldier, writer, and well-known orator. Advocate of a constitutional monarchy but failed to convince Louis XVI of its benefits or to reconcile him with the revolution. **May 1789** Elected to Estates-General as deputy for 3rd Estate. **1791** Appointed president of National Assembly. **Apr 1791** Dies of ill health.

Marie Joseph, Marquis de Lafayette, 1757–1834
Aristocrat, soldier, and hero of the American Revolution. A constitutional monarchist, advocating the restoration of a limited monarchy. **May 1789** Elected to Estates-General as deputy for 2nd Estate. **Aug 1789** Helps draft Declaration of the Rights of Man. **Jul 1789** Appointed commander of revolutionary National Guard. **Jun 1791** Assists Louis XVI's failed escape. **Aug 1792** Leaves France after being declared a traitor to revolution.

Louis Philippe Joseph, Duc d'Orléans, 1747–93
Member of French royal family (Bourbon). Supports revolution. **May 1789** Elected to Estates-General as deputy for 2nd Estate. **Jun 1789** Renounces privileges and joins 3rd Estate. **Jul 1790** Joins National Assembly. **Sep 1792** Given title *Citoyen Égalité* for his role in the revolution.

THE THREE ESTATES OF THE *ANCIEN RÉGIME*

Opening of the Estates-General in Versailles, May 5, 1789

French society before the revolution was divided into three classes, or "Estates". Members of the 3rd Estate, the majority of the population, were denied the privileges of the 1st and 2nd Estates. Revolutionaries, with wide public support, sought to dismantle this system, known as the *ancien régime*.

The 1st Estate included members of the clergy of the Catholic Church (approximately 1% of the population), who owned 20% of the land.
• Exempt from taxation.
• Each year received a payment of 10% of the income of all citizens.

The 2nd Estate included members of the nobility (approximately 2% of the population), the class that owned most of the land.
• Majority paid no tax.
• Entitled to powerful government and army positions.
• Received feudal dues (money and crops) from peasants who farmed their land.

The 3rd Estate included everyone who was not part of the 1st and 2nd Estates, from peasants to middle-class merchants and professionals (approximately 97% of the population).
• All paid taxes, usually high rents, and feudal dues.
• No representation in government.

Meeting of revolutionaries

ROYALISTS

King Louis XVI, 1754–93
Ruler of France. Mismanages economic crisis and fails to realize reforms to ease inequalities. **May 1789** Faced with economic problems, he is forced to call a meeting of the Estates-General (the first for over 100 years), but ignores proposals for reform. **Jun 1791** Plan to escape from France is foiled. **Jan 1793** Tried by National Convention and executed.

Marie Antoinette, 1755–93
Wife of Louis XVI, Queen of France, and Archduchess of Austria. Opposed to reform. Unpopular; regarded as inappropriately extravagant during economic crisis. **Jun 1791** Attempts to escape France with Louis. **Oct 1793** Tried by Revolutionary Tribunal and executed for treason.

Jean-Siffrein Maury, 1746–1817
French cardinal, archbishop of Paris, defender of the *ancien régime*. Known in Paris for his wit and eloquence; a gifted preacher admired by King Louis XVI. **1789** Elected member of Estates-General by clergy. **1789** Remains in France despite desertion by his allies. **1792** Emigrates and finds himself regarded as a martyr to church and king.

THE NATIONAL CONVENTION, 1792–95

On 10 August 1792, a mob forced entry to the Parisian royal palace (the Tuileries), demanding the abolition of the monarchy. The Legislative Assembly then set up by the 3rd Estate decreed the provisional suspension of Louis XVI and the establishment of a National Convention, the first French assembly to be elected by universal male suffrage. The sessions were held in a hall inside the Tuileries.

The main Republican Groups in the National Convention were:

The Mountain (seated on highest benches in assembly)
Radicals dominated by members of the Jacobin Club. Led by Robespierre, who eventually came to dominate the Convention.

The Plain (seated on main floor of assembly)
Moderates opposed to central government and the redistribution of wealth. Dominated by Girondists (from the Gironde region of France), and later by the Mountain, under Robespierre.

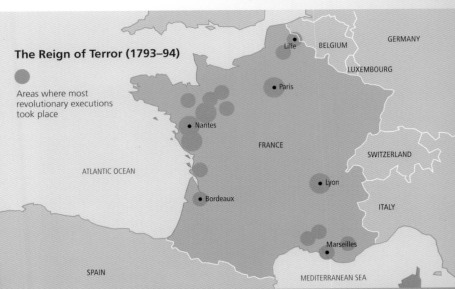

The Reign of Terror (1793–94)

Areas where most revolutionary executions took place

KEY DATES

May 5, 1789	Meeting at Versailles of Estates-General.
Jun 17	National Assembly declared by 3rd Estate.
Jun 20	Tennis Court Oath: 3rd Estate deputies pledge to meet until a constitution is written, despite royal prohibition.
Jul–Aug	The Great Fear: peasantry, hearing a rumor that nobles plan to destroy their crops, ransack estates of nobility.
Jul 14	Storming and fall of Bastille (state prison in Paris).
Aug 5–11	Decrees abolishing feudalism.
Aug 27	Declaration of the Rights of Man approved by National Assembly.
Oct 6	Royal family brought to Paris.
Jun 21, 1791	King flees to Varennes but is captured.
Sep	Constitution of 1791.
Oct 1	Rule of Legislative Assembly begins.
Apr 20, 1792	War of First Coalition (1792–97) in French Revolutionary Wars: France declares war on Austria and Prussia.
Jun 20	Royal family in Tuileries (royal palace) threatened by mob.
Aug 10	Storming of the Tuileries; National Convention established.
Sep	September Massacres: murder of political prisoners.
Sep 21	France declared a Republic.
Oct 2	Committee of General Security established.
Jan 23, 1793	Louis XVI executed.
Mar 10	Revolutionary Tribunal established.
Apr 6	Committee of Public Safety established.
Jun 1793–Jul 1794	The Reign of Terror: "enemies of the state" executed.
May 31–Jun 2, 1793	Coup in Paris by Jacobins (revolutionary political club).
Oct 16	Marie Antoinette executed.
Oct 31	Execution of 31 Girondists.
Apr 5, 1794	Danton executed.
Jun 10	Revolutionary Tribunal powers extended.
Jun 26	Austria defeated by France at Fleurus.
Jul 27	Execution of Robespierre.
Aug 22, 1795	Constitution of 1795 places executive powers in a Directory of Five members (1795–99).
Mar 1796	French invasion of Holy Roman Empire.
Oct 17, 1797	Treaty of Campo Formio; end of War of First Coalition.
1798–1802	War of Second Coalition.
Nov 9, 1799	Napoleon's coup d'état: overthrow of Directory.
Dec 2, 1804	Napoleon proclaims himself Emperor.

LOUIS XVI SUMMONS THE ESTATES GENERAL, 1789

"Beloved and loyal supporters, we require the assistance of our faithful subjects to overcome the difficulties in which we find ourselves concerning the current state of our finances, and to establish, as we so wish, a constant and invariable order in all branches of government that concern the happiness of our subjects and the prosperity of the realm. These great motives have induced us to summon the Assembly of the Estates of all Provinces obedient to us, as much to counsel and assist us in all things placed before it, as to inform us of the wishes and grievances of our people; so that, by means of the mutual confidence and reciprocal love between the sovereign and his subjects, an effective remedy may be brought as quickly as possible to the ills of the State, and abuses of all sorts may be averted and corrected by good and solid means which insure public happiness and restore to us in particular the calm and tranquility of which we have so long been deprived."

Execution of Louis XVI by guillotine in Paris, 1793

THE GUILLOTINE

France descended into chaos during the period June 1793 to July 1794 fearing the threat of counter-revolution from royalist supporters and invasion from foreign powers concerned to halt the spread of revolution. The Reign of Terror earned its name from the high number of executions by guillotine during this period. The Revolutionary Tribunal sentenced thousands to the guillotine. Nobility and commoners, politicians, workers, and intellectuals were executed on suspicion of "crimes against liberty", including Robespierre himself, the main architect of the Reign of Terror. Also referred to as "Madame Guillotine" and "The National Razor", the guillotine in Paris was located in the Place de la Revolution (now Place de la Concorde). Executions by guillotine attracted large crowds of spectators, including parents with children. Programs were sold listing the names of those scheduled to die.

French revolutionary men and women were recognizable by their clothing, in particular the bonnet rouge (red cap) and the sans-culottes (long pants) in striped and tri-color fabric; it became popular to wear peasant clothing because being caught in aristocratic clothes meant beheading

THE DECLARATION OF THE RIGHTS OF MAN AND OF THE CITIZEN, 1789

Approved by the National Assembly of France on August 27, 1789, the Declaration of the Rights of Man and Citizen presented new, radical democratic ideals to countries around the world. Drawing on the ideas of Rousseau and other Enlightenment thinkers, it supported the idea of democratically introduced laws taking precedence over the authority of one ruler, or monarch.

EXTRACT FROM PREAMBLE

The representatives of the French people, organized as a National Assembly, believing that the ignorance, neglect, or contempt of the rights of man are the sole cause of public calamities and of the corruption of governments, have determined to set forth in a solemn declaration the natural, inalienable, and sacred rights of man . . .

ARTICLES

1. Men are born and remain free and equal in rights. Social distinctions may be founded only upon the general good.

2. The aim of all political association is the preservation of the natural and imprescriptible rights of man. These rights are liberty, property, security, and resistance to oppression.

3. The principle of all sovereignty resides essentially in the nation. No body nor individual may exercise any authority which does not proceed directly from the nation.

4. Liberty consists in the freedom to do everything which injures no one else; hence the exercise of the natural rights of each man has no limits except those which assure to the other members of the society the enjoyment of the same rights. These limits can only be determined by law.

5. Law can only prohibit such actions as are hurtful to society. Nothing may be prevented which is not forbidden by law, and no one may be forced to do anything not provided for by law.

6. Law is the expression of the general will. Every citizen has a right to participate personally, or through his representative, in its foundation. It must be the same for all, whether it protects or punishes. All citizens, being equal in the eyes of the law, are equally eligible to all dignities and to all public positions and occupations, according to their abilities, and without distinction except that of their virtues and talents.

7. No person shall be accused, arrested, or imprisoned except in the cases and according to the forms prescribed by law. Any one soliciting, transmitting, executing, or causing to be executed, any arbitrary order, shall be punished. But any citizen summoned or arrested in virtue of the law shall submit without delay, as resistance constitutes an offense.

8. The law shall provide for such punishments only as are strictly and obviously necessary, and no one shall suffer punishment except it be legally inflicted in virtue of a law passed and promulgated before the commission of the offense.

9. As all persons are held innocent until they shall have been declared guilty, if arrest shall be deemed indispensable, all harshness not essential to the securing of the prisoner's person shall be severely repressed by law.

10. No one shall be disquieted on account of his opinions, including his religious views, provided their manifestation does not disturb the public order established by law.

11. The free communication of ideas and opinions is one of the most precious of the rights of man. Every citizen may, accordingly, speak, write, and print with freedom, but shall be responsible for such abuses of this freedom as shall be defined by law.

12. The security of the rights of man and of the citizen requires public military forces. These forces are, therefore, established for the good of all and not for the personal advantage of those to whom they shall be entrusted.

13. A common contribution is essential for the maintenance of the public forces and for the cost of administration. This should be equitably distributed among all the citizens in proportion to their means.

14. All the citizens have a right to decide, either personally or by their representatives, as to the necessity of the public contribution; to grant this freely; to know to what uses it is put; and to fix the proportion, the mode of assessment and of collection and the duration of the taxes.

15. Society has the right to require of every public agent an account of his administration.

16. A society in which the observance of the law is not assured, nor the separation of powers defined, has no constitution at all.

17. Since property is an inviolable and sacred right, no one shall be deprived thereof except where public necessity, legally determined, shall clearly demand it, and then only on condition that the owner shall have been previously and equitably indemnified.

Edmund Burke, English philosopher, in 1790 wrote in his pamphlet *Reflections on the Revolution in France*:

"It is with infinite caution that any man should venture upon pulling down an edifice, which has answered in any tolerable degree for ages the common purposes of society, or on building it up again without having models and patterns of approved utility before his eyes."

Thomas Paine, also of England, in his book that was to become a classic for democratization movements of the 19th-century Europe, *The Rights of Man*, responded to Burke's condemnation of the Revolution:

"Man has no property in men; neither has any generation a property in the generations that have to follow . . . It was . . . against the despotic principles of the government, that the nation revolted. These principles had . . . their origins . . . in the original establishment, many centuries back; and they were to become too deeply rooted to be removed, and the Augean stable of parasites and plunderers too abominably filthy to be cleansed, by anything short of a complete and universal revolution."

Paine was tried and convicted for treason because of his views. He never returned to England; he was also ostracized in the US and died there penniless.

The coronation of Napoleon, 1804

THE RISE OF NAPOLEON BONAPARTE

Born in Corsica in 1768, Napoleon became an artillery officer in the French army in 1785. An ardent supporter of the revolution, and the radical Jacobins, he became a national hero when he defeated the Austrian and Sardinian armies in Italy in 1796. In 1799 he entered a conspiracy to overthrow the Directory of Five, replacing it with a three-man provisional government, with Napoleon at its head as First Consul. By 1804 he had proclaimed himself Emperor of France. In this role he consolidated many reforms of the revolution. The Civil Code introduced in 1804 (the Napoleonic Code) sought to make French law uniform by implementing two key ideas of the revolution: that all men are equal under the law and all people have a right to property. Having centralized the administration of France and crushed any possibility of a counter-revolution, Napoleon set about building his vision of a future united Europe: a new Roman Empire with France at its center.

THE BATTLE OF VALMY, FRANCE – SEPTEMBER 20, 1792

This battle of the French Revolutionary Wars proved to be the turning point of the campaign to reestablish the French king Louis XVI. Anti-revolutionary allied Austrian and Prussian forces under the Duke of Brunswick advanced across the French border. Verdun surrendered on September 3, and Brunswick began his march on Paris. Approaching the defiles of the Argonne he found the Paris road blocked by French general Dumouriez and his troops. The allies forced the northern line of his defense, but the arrival of French general Kellermann to assist Dumouriez, on September 19, led to decisive French artillery action and Brunswick's retreat. On September 21, the day after this victory for France, the French monarchy was abolished and France was declared a Republic.

French under Dumouriez and Kellermann	Prussians under Duke of Brunswick
47,000 troops	35,000 troops
300 casualties	184 casualties

THE FRENCH REVOLUTIONARY WARS, 1792–1802

These wars were undertaken as an effort to defend the French Revolution. They developed into wars to spread the ideas of the Revolution and then, under Napoleon, as wars of conquest to extend the French Empire – the latter generally known as the Napoleonic Wars.

CAUSES

Foreign monarchs, nobles, and clergy feared the spread of revolutionary ideas from France. The foreign powers formed coalitions against France in order to stop the spread of "mob rule".

KEY DATES

1791	Austria and Prussia declare their intention to reinstate King Louis XVI if other powers support them.
Apr 20, 1792	France, in response, declares war on Austria but fails to halt Austrian and Prussian forces as they cross the frontier. Their threat, to raze Paris if the king and his family are harmed, angers the French and contributes to the suspension of the monarchy.
Sep 20	French forces repulse invaders at Valmy, seize the Austrian Netherlands (Belgium), and advance on Frankfurt.

WAR AGAINST FIRST COALITION: AUSTRIA, PRUSSIA, SPAIN, THE UNITED PROVINCES (THE NETHERLANDS), AND BRITAIN

1793	First Coalition formed against France.
Mar 18	French defeated by Austrians at Neerwinden, Belgium.
Jul 23	France loses Mainz (in Germany) to the Prussians.
Apr 6	Committee of Public Safety established to deal with emergency. Draft of males 18–25 years decreed, raising a vast army.
By end 1793	Allies driven from France; France takes the offensive.
By 1795	France has defeated allies in Germany, Austria, and the Netherlands.
1796	Napoleon assumes command of Italian campaign, taking Sardinia (May 1796).
1797	Treaty of Campo Formio: Austria forced to cede Austrian Netherlands.
Aug 1798	Britain's naval triumph under Admiral Nelson at Aboukir, Egypt.

WAR AGAINST SECOND COALITION: BRITAIN, RUSSIA, OTTOMAN EMPIRE, NAPLES, PORTUGAL, AND AUSTRIA

1798	France's establishment of republican regimes in Rome, Switzerland (the Helvetic Republic), and Italy (the Parthenopean Republic) prompts creation of Second Coalition.
Nov 1799	Napoleon returns to France from Egypt and becomes First Consul.
1800–02	Second Coalition, weakened from Russia's withdrawal, suffers defeats and ultimately makes peace with France: Austrians crushed at Marengo (Jun 14) agree peace treaty (1801), forcing Austria out of the war; Britain, though victorious at Malta (Sep 1800), Egypt (Aug 1801), and Copenhagen (Apr 1801), consents to peace in 1802 restoring all conquered lands to France.

France and other European countries continue their conflict in the Napoleonic Wars until Napoleon's defeat and the restoration of the Bourbon monarchy in France in 1815.

The battle of Valmy, 1792

The Latin American Revolutions

In 1808 the Spanish Empire covered most of south and central America, as well as much of north America. Spain tightly controlled trade, immigration, and political power, and gained enormous wealth from the colonies she ruled. Similarly, Portugal owned and ran Brazil. But within two decades the whole of the Latin American subcontinent was independent of European control, and Spain only owned the islands of Cuba and Puerto Rico. Although events in Mexico and Brazil were separate, most of Spanish America found itself acting together to bring about independence, then pulling itself apart in civil wars.

General José de San Martín leading the revolutionary troops at the battle of Chacabuco, February 12, 1817

CAUSES

Desire for Autonomy Spain had a tight control on her colonies. All the top positions, whether in political administration, the army, or the church, were held by Spaniards appointed by Spain. Similarly, the all-important trade was controlled by Spain, and the colonies were only allowed to trade externally with Spanish merchants. Creoles – American-born Spanish – resented this control and wanted more political and commercial autonomy. Many creoles did not at first want to extend this to total independence from Spain.

Enlightenment Thinking Ideals of liberty and democracy inspired some of the revolutionary leaders, particularly Simón Bolívar.

The "Age of Revolution" The examples of the American, French, and Haitian revolutions showed that changes could be achieved by popular uprisings.

Napoleonic Wars The main trigger for the revolutions was Napoleon Bonaparte's invasion of the Iberian Peninsula (Portugal and Spain). The Spanish king, Ferdinand VII, was deposed and a French Bonaparte king put in his place. To Spanish colonials, this meant there was a power vacuum. They did not consider they owed loyalty to the new puppet king, so who had authority over them? The disenchanted creole elites decided that they could take control for themselves.

CONSEQUENCES

• The creation of independent nations in Latin America, originally covering vast territories but later dividing into the modern countries.

• Despite Bolívar's hopes, the new nations were not liberal democracies. Within a few years most were controlled by dictators from the creole elites.

• Power struggles led to fighting and civil wars, sometimes almost immediately after the wars of independence.

• The new constitutions recognized racial equality in law, but did nothing to end racial discrimination or to resolve the social tensions between rich and poor.

• The indigenous populations were worse off than before. While they no longer had to pay tribute and give free labor, as equals in law they now had to pay taxes and they lost the protection Spain had finally given to their communal lands. Within a few years most of these were lost to whites.

• The USA instituted the Monroe Doctrine, a declaration that it would not accept any European interference in the Americas.

REVOLUTIONARY LEADERS

Francisco de Miranda (Sebastián Francisco de Miranda y Rodriguez), 1750–1816
Venezuelan. 1771 Joins Spanish army. 1780 Serves in America, supporting revolutionaries against Britain. 1791 Takes part in French Revolution. 1810 Sets up revolutionary junta in Venezuela. Jul 1811 Declares independence. Jul 1812 After several military defeats, surrenders to Spain. Considered a traitor by Bolívar and others, is handed over to Spanish army. 1816 Dies in prison in Spain.

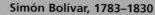

Simón Bolívar, 1783–1830
Venezuelan. Inspirational leader. 1810 Joins the revolutionary junta. 1812 Flees after de Miranda surrenders to Spain. 1813 Invades Venezuela, declaring the Second Republic. Given name "The Liberator". 1814 Forced out of Venezuela, embarks on failed raids until revolutionary tide turns. 1819–24 Directs successful campaigns in the north. 1819 President of republic of Gran Colombia. 1824 Becomes dictator of Peru. 1826 His dream of enlightened, liberal federation crumbles as Gran Colombia begins to fall apart. 1830 Resigns.

José Francisco de San Martín, 1778–1850
Argentinean. Brilliant general. Forms the disciplined, professional Army of the Andes. 1817 Defeats royalists at Chacabuco in Chile. Turns down position of Chilean head of state. Apr 5, 1818 Wins decisive battle of Maipo, liberating Chile. 1820 Leads invasion of Peru. July 1821 Enters Lima; declares Peruvian independence. 1822 Following secret talks with Bolívar, resigns and leaves for France.

Antonio José de Sucre, 1795–1830
Venezuelan soldier. 1818 Becomes general in Bolívar's army. 1822 Wins battle of Pichincha, Ecuador. 1824 Is chief commander at conclusive victory of Ayacucho, Peru. 1825 Becomes president of Bolivia. 1828 Resigns. 1830 Heads constitutional convention which fails to hold Gran Colombia together. 1830 Ambushed and killed, probably by a political rival.

Bernardo O'Higgins (Riquelme), 1778–1842
Chilean. Illegitimate son of Irish former governor. Nov 1813 Takes command of Chilean forces. 1814 Overwhelmed at Rancagua, flees across the Andes. Joins San Martín. 1817

PHASE 1

1808	France, under Napoleon, invades Spain, imposing own king.
1810	Creoles opposing French rule set up juntas (government committees) in Argentina, Chile, Venezuela, and New Granada (modern Colombia).
1811	Venezuela announces independence.
1812	Venezuelan revolutionaries defeated by Spanish royalist forces.
1813	Simón Bolívar frees Venezuela.
1814	Ferdinand VII reclaims Spain and Spanish armies go on the offensive in the Americas, reclaiming Chile from the rebels.
1815	Royalists under General Pablo Morillo regain control of all of Spanish South America except for the Argentine provinces; many Chilean revolutionaries flee there; Bolívar forced into exile.

PHASE 2

1816	Argentina declares independence; Bolívar returns to Venezuela to lead rebellion.
1817	Under General Jose de San Martín, the revolutionary Army of the Andes crosses the Andes from Argentina into Chile and on Feb 12 wins the battle of Chacabuco.
1818	In the north, Bolívar takes part of Venezuela; in the south, San Martín wins the battle of Maipo and liberates Chile.
1819	Bolívar wins the battle of Boyacá and wins independence for New Granada in the north; he forms Republic of Gran Colombia (Venezuela, Colombia, Ecuador) and moves some forces south into Peru.
1820	San Martín moves north and invades Peru.
1821	Bolívar wins battle of Carabobo, completing the liberation of Venezuela.
1822	General Antonio Jose de Sucre wins the battle of Pichincha, freeing Quito from Spain; Bolívar and San Martín meet at Guayaquil, following which San Martín retires.
1824	Bolívar and Sucre win battles of Junín and Ayacucho in Peru, ending the wars of independence.
1826	Last Spanish garrisons surrender.

BRAZIL

Following Napoleon's invasion of Portugal in 1807, the Portuguese royal family fled to Brazil. When King John VI eventually returned to Portugal in 1821, his son, Pedro, stayed in Brazil as prince regent. A movement for independence began to grow in Brazil after the revolutions in other Latin American countries. Nationalist and separatist feelings deepened when the Portuguese parliament tried to strengthen its authority over Brazil. Pedro took control of the nationalist movement before it could reach a violent, revolutionary stage, and in September 1822 declared Brazil's independence, with himself as emperor.

Helps defeat royalists and is appointed by San Martín to administer Chile as director-general. **1818** Helps win victory at Maipo. Tries to create an unpopular constitution, giving him dictatorial powers. **1823** After popular uprisings against him, resigns and retires to Peru.

Ramón Freire Serrano, 1787–1851
Chilean. **1811** Joins revolutionary junta's army. **1814** After defeat at Rancagua, takes refuge in Argentina and joins San Martín. **1818** Leads an army unit in the liberation of Chile. **1822** Becomes rallying point for opposition to O'Higgins. **1823** Appointed new director-general. Introduces many reforms such as abolition of slavery. **1827** Retires but in period of civil wars spends years in exile.

Miguel Hidalgo, 1753–1811
Mexican creole priest. **1810** Organizes conspiracy for a popular uprising. Launches the first wave of Mexican wars of independence. Uses religious language to inspire rebellion. **1811** Captured, excommunicated, executed. His head is put on public display.

Battles of Liberation

⊗ Battle

——— Advance of Bolívar and his forces

- - - - Advance of San Martín

MEXICO

The only country to experience popular uprisings, the independence movement in Mexico was at first led by revolutionaries who wanted to see a more equal society. The first leader, the priest Miguel Hidalgo, was executed in 1810, but rebellion continued under another priest, José María Morelos y Pavón, who took control of parts of the country before he was captured and executed in 1815. Vicente Guerrero then took the lead. In 1820 an army mutiny in Spain forced the king to accept a liberal constitution. Conservative Mexicans, led by Agustin de Iturbide (once a rebel, later a royalist), rejected this and conspired to bring about independence. Promising certain rights, they won over the rebels, and declared independence in 1821.

Soldiers of the newly independent Mexican state, wearing distinctive Mexican, rather than Spanish, uniforms

THE AFTERMATH

The new countries soon found themselves torn apart by regional interests. In some cases this led to civil wars, in other cases the large territories and federations split, forming several new countries. Central America separated from Mexico in 1823, then split into five new countries: El Salvador, Costa Rica, Honduras, Nicaragua, and Guatemala. In 1828 Uruguay became independent of the Argentine provinces, which then divided into Paraguay and Argentina. Finally, in 1830 Gran Colombia divided into Ecuador, New Granada (Colombia and Panama), and Venezuela.

The battle of Maipo, April 5, 1818

The Zulu Civil Wars

Originally a small tribe of the Nguni people of southern Africa, the Zulus created a great empire. Although it was independent for less than 100 years, its fearless warriors gained a world-wide reputation. This fame was partly because the Zulus were one of the few African people to defeat European colonizers in battle (e.g. beating the British at Isandlwana, January 22, 1879), but also because the empire was forged through vicious civil wars with other tribes and clans of the Nguni. Later, after the great but brutal king Shaka Zulu had created his nation, there were several bloody battles between rivals for his throne.

A group of Zulus photographed c. 1880

CAUSES

1. First Civil War (Ndwandwe–Zulu War) Shaka, ill-treated as a child, took revenge as an adult by massacring the clans he held a grudge against, and expanding his rule through civil wars against other tribes.

2. Later Civil Wars Royal brothers or cousins fought over who would inherit the kingdom or would have control over parts of the kingdom.

CONSEQUENCES

1. Shaka established a great, powerful nation, and caused the *Mfecane* (scattering), a disturbance throughout southern Africa as tribes tried to escape the Zulus by migrating away, fighting their own battles for new territory.

2. Zulu autonomy and land began to be eroded as each side in the later civil wars gave concessions to either the Boers or the British colonizers in southern Africa in return for help.

SHAKA'S MILITARY INNOVATIONS

• Previous warfare between southern African tribes involved a great deal of posturing and ritual threatening, but not a lot of bloodshed. Shaka wanted to kill, and he taught his regiments to fight to the death – usually the enemy's.

• Before Shaka, the main weapon was the *assegai*, a light throwing spear. Shaka said this was a waste of a weapon, and he invented a broad-bladed stabbing spear, the *iklwa*, named for the sound it made going into the body.

• He created larger shields, and trained his warriors to hook them under the enemy's shield, pull it away, and expose the ribs for a spear thrust.

• He developed the *impondo zannkhomo* or beast horns' formation, where the "chest" attacked in full frontal assault, and "horns" on either side outflanked and surrounded the enemy. The "loins" were kept in reserve.

THE CIVIL WARS

1817–19	Civil War (Ndwandwe–Zulu War). Begins when the Ndwandwe tribe kill Shaka's mentor Dingiswayo. In 1819 Shaka's tactics defeat the larger force of Ndwandwe at Gqokli Hill.
1820	Fighting breaks out again. Shaka ambushes and defeats the Ndwandwe at the Mhlatuze River, inflicting a heavy defeat. He then continues conquests to forge his empire.
1828	Shaka is stabbed to death by his half-brothers Dingane and Mhlangana. Dingane takes the throne and kills most of his relatives as well as Shaka's closest aids.
1838–40	Mpande–Dingane Civil War. The one surviving half-brother, Mpande, seeks help from the Boers in return for land in Natal, and attacks Dingane. In 1840 Mpande wins decisive battle in the Maqongqo Hills, northern Zululand.
Dec 2, 1856	Battle of the Princes. Mpande's oldest sons, Cetshwayo and Mbuyazi, are bitter rivals and meet in battle at Ndondakasuka on the Tugela River. Cetshwayo pins his enemies against the river bank and kills about 20,000, including Mbuyazi.
1878–79	Anglo–Zulu Wars. Despite inflicting a rare defeat on British colonial forces at Isandlwana (Jan 22, 1879), Zulus are finally defeated at Ulundi (Jul 4, 1879). Britain takes Cetshwayo captive and divides Zululand into 13 small chiefdoms, which immediately begin in-fighting.
1883–84	Civil War. Cetshwayo returns from exile to unite the chiefs, but cannot reconcile his supporters to his cousin, Zibhebhu.
Jul 21, 1883	After initial setbacks, Zibhebhu rallies and attacks Cetshwayo's camp at Ulundi. The king flees, and dies in 1884.
Jun 5, 1884	Cetshwayo's son Dinuzulu defeats Zibhebhu at Entshaneni in the Lebombo Mountains. Dinuzulu becomes paramount chief under British rule.

Shaka's Battle Formation

"Chest" – Veteran warriors would draw the enemy inside the pincer formation, then attack

Enemy

"Horns" – Formations on either side, consisting of young, fast warriors. These would flank the enemy, trying to remain out of sight, then attack by surprise from the sides and rear

Zulu Army

"Loins" – Older warriors held in reserve

THE WARRING KINGS

Mpande

Shaka, c. 1787–1828
Illegitimate son of Zulu chief Senzangakona, taunted as a child over his odd physical appearance and his illegitimacy. Found friendship with the Mthethwa chief Dingiswayo. **1816** Claims Zulu leadership. **1817** Embarks upon wars of conquest, creating an empire dominating southeastern Africa.

Mpande, 1798–1872
Ignored by his brother Dingane as being weak and incompetent, but managed to take and keep the throne, ruling well for many years.

Cetshwayo, 1826–Feb 1884
Won some victories but was ultimately defeated by the British, and was no longer able to hold the Zulus together.

1848 Revolutions

In February 1848 French king Louis Philippe fled in panic after protesters demanded political rights. This triggered a wave of urban, middle class revolutions in Europe. During this "springtime of peoples", frightened governments immediately promised social and political reforms. However most rulers soon regained their nerves and clamped down on unrest. In the long term, very little changed. It has been called Europe's "turning point which failed to turn".

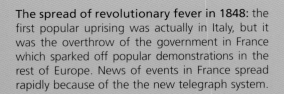

A mob burning the royal carriages at the Chateau d'Eu, Normandy, France, February 24, 1848

The spread of revolutionary fever in 1848: the first popular uprising was actually in Italy, but it was the overthrow of the government in France which sparked off popular demonstrations in the rest of Europe. News of events in France spread rapidly because of the the new telegraph system.

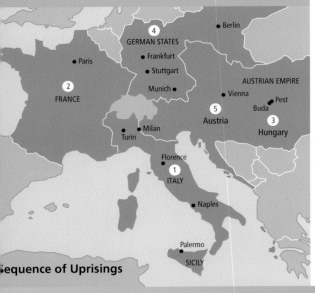

Sequence of Uprisings

CAUSES

• Following several poor harvests, 1847 saw a great depression. Poverty and unemployment added to social tensions caused by industrialization and population growth. Europe was ready to explode.

• The immediate spark for many uprisings was the example of France. The French people had once again shown that it was possible to achieve a change in government and political structure.

• Different forms of nationalism were growing. Italians wanted to free themselves from Austria, and then unite. Germans wanted a progressive confederation of states. Hungarians and Czechs – part of the Austrian Empire – at first just wanted some autonomy.

• Liberals wanted modest, non-violent political changes such as a free press, elected assemblies, written constitutions.

• Radicals wanted changes that were thought to be extreme – votes for all (men); some sort of welfare; giving land to peasants; social justice. Many radicals supported violent revolution.

CONSEQUENCES

• The only regime change was in France, where the Second Republic was declared in 1848. This lasted only until 1851, when president Louis Bonaparte launched a coup d'état, and became Emperor Napoleon III.

• Austrian Chancellor Metternich resigned and Emperor Ferdinand abdicated in favor of his nephew, Franz Josef.

• Some social changes survived in France, where the republic introduced the vote for all men, and enforced the emancipation of slaves in its colonies. Peasants in Austria and Prussia saw improvements as feudal burdens and serfdom were removed.

• Most political concessions, such as the elected assemblies in Germany and Austria, were revoked. But limited constitutions survived in Prussia and Sardinia.

• Germany and Austria became more, rather than less, autocratic, introducing secret police and censorship. Nationalism there developed into a conservative, not a liberal, ideal. More than one million Germans emigrated, particularly the educated bourgeois.

REVOLUTIONARIES

Armand Sigismond Auguste Barbès, 1809–70 and Auguste Blanqui, 1805–81
French, "professional" revolutionaries. Main aim: to establish a more just society. 1835 Form an illegal secret society together. Mar 10, 1836 Imprisoned for revolutionary activities. May 12, 1839 Attempted coup d'état fails; imprisoned again. Mar 1848 Become enemies after Blanqui is falsely accused of betraying his colleagues. May 15, 1848 Feeling revolution has not gone far enough, they lead attempt to declare a new, more radical government. (Both possibly only get involved to stop the other becoming pre-eminent). Arrested and imprisoned again. Spend rest of their lives agitating for change.

Robert Blum, 1807–48
German radical. Main aims: radical reforms such as full male suffrage, abolition of all privileges. Opposes violent insurrection. Mar 1848 Helps organize and is elected to the first German National Assembly (GNA). Oct 1848 Supports Viennese revolution as representative of GNA. Nov 9, 1848 Executed by Austrian government after defeat of rebels.

Giuseppe Garibaldi, 1807–82
Italian nationalist general. Main aim: a united republican Italy. 1834 Flees Italy after failure of "Young Italy" revolution. Fights for emancipation movements in South America. 1848–9 Gains renown in Piedmontese struggle against Austria and as military leader of short-lived revolutionary Roman Republic. 1860 Leads "Red Shirts" liberation of Sicily and southern Italy, helping bring about Italian unification. 1874 Becomes member of Italian parliament.

Lajos (Louis) Kossuth, 1802–94
Hungarian lawyer, journalist. Main aims: abolition of feudalism, modest nationalist desire for a separate Hungarian parliament within Austrian Empire. 1837–40 Imprisoned for his views. 1840s Publishes influential nationalist newspaper. Mar 3, 1848 Speech demanding self-government launches social and nationalist revolution. Sep 1848 Leads Hungarian forces after Austria and Russia invade. Apr 14, 1849 Declares full Hungarian independence. Aug 1849 Escapes to England after Hungarian defeat.

The Native American Revolts

Also called the Plains Indian Wars or the Sioux Wars, the revolts of 1854–90 were the most significant opposition by Native American groups to the march of the USA across the continent. They were the desperate attempt by tribes on the plains of Wyoming, Minnesota, Montana, and the Dakotas to keep their traditional lifestyles on their customary lands. There were other last-ditch resistance movements by Native Americans in the far west and in the southwest, but the Indian Wars are said to have ended with the massacre of Sioux at Wounded Knee in 1890.

The battle of the Little Bighorn, Montana, June 25, 1876; the retreat of the US 7th Cavalry battalions under Major Marcus Reno as seen by the Sioux artist Amos Bad Heart Buffalo

CAUSES

• In pursuit of its "manifold destiny" to expand across the continent, by 1848 the USA had gained all its current continental territories, but the only area not yet touched by white settlers was the Great Plains. First, pioneers heading to the far west clashed with Plains tribes, then farmers, ranchers, and miners – protected by soldiers – began to settle on the Plains themselves.

• US policy was to move Native Americans onto reservations where they would be taught farming and be educated, so would no longer be a "problem" standing in the way of "progress". Used to a nomadic, buffalo-hunting lifestyle, the Plains tribes violently resisted this policy as long as possible.

• Often, reservation land was not good enough to support the tribes. If supplies were not provided, bands would leave the reservation. At this point they would be considered to be in revolt.

CONSEQUENCES

• All Native American peoples lost the struggle and were forced to give up their lands and lifestyles.

• By 1880 Native Americans were squeezed into six percent of their original land. The reservations were often on barren land, unable to support farms. The tribes usually sank into poverty, despair, or alcoholism.

• Any Native Americans who resisted the reservations were considered "hostile" and could be killed.

The massacre at Wounded Knee; trigger-happy troops of the 7th Cavalry, worried about the revolutionary potential of the Ghost Dance movement and itching for revenge for the Little Bighorn disaster, open fire on Big Foot's band

Native American Revolts
⊗ Battle   ○ Fort
----- Bozeman Trail
----- Oregon Trail

Is it wrong for me to love my own? Is it wicked for me because my skin is red? Because I am Sioux? Because I was born where my father lived? Because I would die for my people and my country?

Sitting Bull

NATIVE AMERICAN RESISTERS

Sitting Bull, c. 1831–90
Hunkpapa Sioux. Respected medicine man (spiritual advisor) and leader. **Jun 1876** Summons the muster of tribes at Little Bighorn. **1877** Leads his band to temporary refuge in Canada. **Jul 20, 1881** Unable to maintain traditional lifestyle, surrenders in Dakota Territory. **1885** Tours with Buffalo Bill Cody's Wild West Show. **Dec 15, 1890** Killed when Indian police attempt to arrest him to stop the Ghost Dance movement.

Crazy Horse, c. 1840–77
Oglala Sioux. A famous warrior, and renowned for his charity to the poor. **c. 1865** Selected by tribal elders as one of the most honorable young men. **1866 and 1876** Fights or leads at victories over Fetterman, at the Rosebud and at Little Bighorn. **Sep 1877** Facing starvation, he leads his 900-strong band to surrender. **Sep 6, 1877** Arrested over a misunderstanding, killed in the scuffle. *There are no verified photographs of Crazy Horse. An enigmatic recluse, he did not attend treaty talks, and apart from battles, had no contact with white men until the last days of his life on the reservation. Even then, he kept his distance as much as possible.*

Red Cloud, 1822–1909
Oglala/Brulé Sioux. Not a chief, but organized many attacks in "Red Cloud's War", successfully opposing the Bozeman Trail forts. Adept at dealing with government officials. **1875** Anticipates inevitable defeat, so advocates selling land for best possible price. **1876** Accepts reservation. **1880** Leads Sioux protests against loss of reservation land and other injustices.

Spotted Elk (Big Foot), c. 1825–90
Miniconjou Sioux; half-brother of Sitting Bull. Gains renown for settling disputes. Used diplomatic skills in discussions with US government. **1877** Placed on reservation, becomes one of first Sioux to farm and grow corn. **Dec 1890** After Sitting Bull's death, fears trouble and leads his band to Red Cloud's reservation. **Dec 29, 1890** Intercepted by soldiers at Wounded Knee. Killed with up to 300 people.

Aug 18, 1854	After rising tensions, fighting breaks out near Fort Laramie, Wyoming.
1862–64	Sioux Uprising (Santee War), Minnesota. Little Crow leads a violent rebellion by despairing reservation Santee. They are captured and 38 are executed.
1864–65	Colorado War. Starving Cheyenne and Arapaho leave their reservations. On Nov 29, 1864 local militia massacre about 200 people at Black Kettle's peaceable village at Sand Creek.
1866–68	Red Cloud's War.
1866	Red Cloud attacks forts guarding the Bozeman Trail to gold-strike in Montana. Dec 21, 1866, Crazy Horse kills Captain Fetterman and his 80 men near Fort Kearny, Wyoming. Apr 29, 1868, in the Fort Laramie Treaty, the US abandons the Bozeman Trail forts and grants lands to the Sioux "forever".
Nov 27, 1868	Battle of the Washita. George Armstrong Custer attacks Black Kettle's camp and forces all Cheyenne onto reservations.
1870s	Buffalo hunters, often using the new railroads, decimate the herds.
1874–75	Red River War. Starving Comanche and other southern plains tribes leave their reservations and are hunted down.
1874	Custer discovers gold in the Black Hills. Sioux refuse to sell the land, so US government revokes Fort Laramie Treaty and orders all Indians to settle on reservations.
1876–77	Black Hills War/Great Sioux War/ Little Bighorn Campaign. US army moves to settle Sioux on reservations. Sitting Bull summons an inter-tribal meeting. Sioux, Cheyenne, and Arapaho gather at Rosebud Creek, Montana.
Jun 1876	Sitting Bull has a vision of white soldiers falling, a prophecy of Sioux victory.
Jun 17	Crazy Horse leads up to 1,500 warriors who halt General George Crook's 1,000-strong force at the battle of the Rosebud.
Jun 25	Crazy Horse defeats Custer at the Little Bighorn.
1878–89	Cheyenne War. Unable to survive on their reservation, Cheyenne attempt to return to their homelands in the northern plains. Many are killed and the survivors surrender.
1889	The Ghost Dance movement, promising a return to traditional life, spreads rapidly. It is banned, but widely practiced.
Dec 29, 1890	Massacre at Wounded Knee. Mostly unarmed, about 300 men, women, and children of the band of Spotted Elk (Big Foot), Sitting Bull's half-brother, are killed by soldiers. 13 US soldiers are killed, probably by friendly fire. The last major confrontation between US forces and Native Americans.
1890	The frontier is declared "closed".

US ARMY LEADERS

Lt. Colonel George Armstrong Custer, 1839–76
Cavalry commander. Flamboyant and over-confident. **1861–65** Distinguishes himself in Federal cavalry during the Civil War. Wins temporary war-time promotion to general. **Nov 27, 1868** At Washita River, forces the southern Cheyenne onto reservations. **1874** Heads army expedition into Black Hills, Dakota; discovers gold. **May 17, 1876** Leads 7th Cavalry to disaster at battle of the Little Bighorn, where he is killed.

General Nelson A. Miles, 1839–1925
Soldier who made his reputation during the Civil War. **1874–75** Oversees victories over southern plains tribes. **1876** Promises fair treatment to Crazy Horse if he will surrender. **1877** Captures Nez Perce chief Joseph who has led his tribe on a 1,700-mile journey from Oregon towards Canada. **Sep 1886** Accepts surrender of Apache leader Geronimo. **1990** Acts to suppress Ghost Dance.

THE BATTLE OF THE LITTLE BIGHORN, MONTANA – JUNE 25, 1876

The most famous battle of all the Indian Wars, and the most notorious defeat of the US cavalry, is also known as "Custer's Last Stand".

Leading the 7th Cavalry, George Armstrong Custer was looking for Native Americans who were not on reservations. When his scouts sighted a massive band at the Little Bighorn river, Custer did not wait for his infantry to catch up. He thought the Indians would flee rather than fight openly, and, he was probably keen to take any possible glory for himself.

Custer split his forces into three to try a pincer movement, but Major Reno's and Captain Benteen's groups were forced back. Custer's section advanced, and was wiped out. Reno and Benteen escaped the next day.

In response, the US government flooded the area with soldiers. In less than a year, the surviving Sioux had to flee or surrender.

US Army under Custer	Sioux, Cheyenne, Arapaho, under Crazy Horse and others
263 cavalry, scouts, civilians	c. 2,000
263 killed	unknown: c. 45–200 killed

"Commanche", the only survivor of Custer's detachment at the battle of the Little Bighorn

The Ghost Dance: desperate Sioux adopted the dance, hoping it would free the world from the white man

EXTRACT FROM THE TREATY OF FORT LARAMIE, 1868

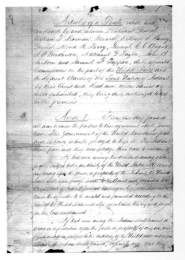

ARTICLE I
From this day forward all war between the parties to this agreement shall for ever cease. The government of the United States desires peace, and its honor is hereby pledged to keep it. The Indians desire peace, and they now pledge their honor to maintain it …

ARTICLE II
The United States agrees that the following district of country, to wit, viz: commencing on the east bank of the Missouri river where the 46th parallel of north latitude crosses the same, thence along low-water mark down said east bank to a point opposite where the northern line of the State of Nebraska strikes the river, thence west across said river, and along the northern line of Nebraska to the 104th degree of longitude west from Greenwich …shall be and the same is, set apart for the absolute and undisturbed use and occupation of the Indians herein named …and the United States now solemnly agrees that no persons, except those herein designated and authorized so to do, and except such officers, agents, and employees of the government as may be authorized to enter upon Indian reservations in discharge of duties enjoined by law, shall ever be permitted to pass over, settle upon, or reside in the territory described in this article …

The American Civil War

Also known as the War Between the States, the Civil War was fought because of slavery. Southern states attempted to break away from the Union when they feared that the government would take away states' rights to self-determination, particularly their right to decide on slavery.

Dead Union soldiers on the battlefield at Gettysburg, Pennsylvania, July 1863

CAUSES

• The economies of the southern states depended upon the institution of slavery whereas a growing number of northerners agreed that slavery was morally wrong.

• Southern states feared that the Federal government would insist all new territories opening up in the west of the country would be slave-free. This would mean that slave-owning states would become a minority in the Senate and might be forced to emancipate.

• Southern states held that they had a constitutional right to secede from the Union and form their own nation, the Confederate States of America (1861). Northern states held that this was unconstitutional, and President Lincoln proclaimed that it was his solemn duty to preserve the Union.

CONSEQUENCES

• Abolition of slavery. Lincoln's 1862 Emancipation Proclamation was made while war was still raging, but was ratified in the 13th Amendment in 1865.

• Racism remained a powerful force in the South. Bitterly resentful, many Southerners took out their feelings on the newly freed African American population, ensuring that it would be decades before civil rights were shared equally in the nation.

• Because the Confederate commerce raiders, or pirates, were attacking Union ships, traders around the world stopped using American ships to carry their goods. The US merchant navy never regained the traffic it lost.

KEY FEDERAL FIGURES

Abraham Lincoln, 1809–65
Lawyer, politician. Considered to be one of the greatest presidents. Powerful, eloquent orator. Born in Kentucky. **1847** Becomes member of House of Representatives. **1856** Joins the newly formed Republican Party which is opposed to slavery. **1860** Elected president. **Sep 22, 1862** Makes the Emancipation Proclamation. **Nov 19, 1863** Gives the inspirational Gettysburg Address – "this government of the people, by the people, for the people …". Quick to fire vacillating generals, he is only happy when he settles on the tenacious Grant as overall commander. **Nov 1864** Re-elected. **Apr 15, 1865** Assassinated.

David Glasgow Farragut, 1801–70
Sailor, born in Tennessee. **1861** Appointed commander of Western Blockade Squadron. **Apr 1862** Captures New Orleans. **Jul 1862** Promoted to rear admiral, the US Navy's first admiral. **Aug 1864** Leads naval attack on Mobile, saying "Damn the torpedoes! Full speed ahead!" **1866** Promoted to new rank of full admiral

Ulysses Simpson Grant, 1822–85
Soldier, born in Ohio. **Feb 1862** Captures Fort Donelson, demanding "Unconditional surrender", which becomes his nickname. **Apr 1862** Wins Shiloh, takes command of Western Armies. **Mar 1864** Appointed general-in-chief, takes command in the East. Determined and decisive, forces overall victory. **1867–68** Becomes secretary of war. **1869** Elected president, serving until 1877. Finishes his memoirs four days before dying of throat cancer.

George Brinton McClellan, 1826–85
Soldier, born in Philadelphia. **1861** After minor early success, is appointed general-in-chief of the army. Spends months reorganizing the army and only advances when Lincoln becomes fed up with his delays. **Jun 1862** Wins most of the battles of the Seven Days but, over-cautious and over-estimating enemy strength, still retreats.

KEY CONFEDERATE FIGURES

Jefferson Davis, 1808–89
Politician, born in Kentucky. **1845** First enters Congress. **1846–48** Resigns in order to fight in Mexican War. **1848** Elected senator for Mississippi. **Jan 1861** Resigns to join the secessionists. **Feb 1861** Elected president of the Confederate States of America. Succeeds in holding Confederacy together through the war, and allows his best generals to do their job, but interferes with others. Imprisoned for two years after the war.

Nathan Bedford Forrest, 1821–77
Cavalryman, born in Tennessee. A self-made man, becoming wealthy from slave-dealing and cotton farming. One of the few senior leaders not professionally trained. **1862** Makes a daring escape from Fort Donelson before it surrenders. **1863** Leads several raids into Union territory. **1864** Blamed for the massacre of black troops trying to surrender at Fort Pillow. After the war founds the Ku Klux Klan.

Thomas Jonathan (Stonewall) Jackson, 1824–63
Soldier, born in Virginia. Called a "blue-eyed killer". **1851** Appointed professor of artillery tactics at Virginia Military Institute. **Jul 1861** Stands firm in defence at First Bull Run, gaining the nickname "Stonewall". **Nov 1861–Jun 1862** Wins several battles against superior forces in the Shenandoah Valley, tying up enemy forces. **Aug 1862** More brilliant campaigning culminates in victory at Second Bull Run. **May 2, 1863** Leads another excellent flanking maneuver at Chancellorsville, but is shot by friendly fire and dies days later.

Robert Edward Lee, 1807–70
Soldier, born in Virginia. Son of Revolutionary War hero Henry (Light Horse Harry) Lee. **1852–55** Appointed Superintendent of West Point military college. **1861** When war breaks out he rejects offer of command of Union army in order to remain loyal to his home state. A great general, he wins several victories in the East and when forced on the defensive manages to stave off total defeat until outflanked and overwhelmed.

WAR IN THE WEST

The Union attempted to open up routes into the South via the Mississippi River and Tennessee. Having taken New Orleans and Memphis in 1862, the Union was able to sail both upstream and downstream along the Mississippi, finally taking control of the river after the fall of Vicksburg in 1863. This then divided the Confederacy into two. In May 1864 Sherman went on the offensive from Tennessee and launched his March to the Sea, driving through Georgia. He was then able to swing north to link with Grant's eastern armies.

1862

Feb 6 and 14–16	Forts Henry and Donelson: Union take strategic forts
Apr 6–7	Shiloh: Union just manages to beat off attack and keeps strategic advantage

1863

Jul	Vicksburg falls to Union
Sep 19–20	Chickamauga: Only major Confederate victory in the West temporarily beats Union back
Nov 24–25	Chattanooga: Union reclaims position in Tennessee

1864

May 4–Sep 2	Atlanta campaign: Sherman advances through the South
Dec 15–16	Nashville: Union victory protects Sherman's back

WAR ON THE WATER

As well as an attempted blockade of the South (the Confederate coastline stretched for 3,500 miles), the Union navy attacked forts and ports to take control of the coast. Confederate commerce raiders attacked Northern ships anywhere in the world, leading to naval battles off the coast of France.

WAR IN THE EAST

Huge armies maneuvered, advanced, and retreated, clashing in massive, bloody battles as they tried to capture the other side's capital city – Washington DC for the Union and Richmond for the Confederacy. If they lost a battle they simply withdrew to well-defended safe positions. The South was unable to build on early successes, and Lee was defeated badly when he tried to reverse the flow of war and invade the North. Once Grant took control of the Northern forces, he never gave Lee a chance to catch his breath, and pressed on until the exhausted Confederate forces were surrounded and finally beaten.

1861

Apr 12	The Confederacy fires upon the Union-held Fort Sumter in Charleston harbor, starting the war
Jul 21	First Bull Run (Manassas): Confederates repulse Union

1862

Jun 25–Jul 1	The Seven Days: Lee leads Union army away from Richmond
Aug 29–30	Second Bull Run: Confederates gain the initiative
Sep 17	Antietam (Sharpsburg): Confederate invasion of Maryland beaten back
Dec 13	Fredericksburg: Union advance repulsed

1863

May 1–4	Chancellorsville: Union attack repulsed
Jul 1–3	Gettysburg: Confederate invasion of Pennsylvania repulsed

1864

May 5–6	Wilderness: A drawn battle but from now on the Union does not retreat
Jun 19	Petersburg campaign begins as Grant moves to pin down Lee's armies and cut off their supply lines

1865

Apr 2	After months of trench warfare and several battles, Lee is forced to abandon Petersburg and then Richmond; he is now in full retreat
Apr 9	Harried, short of men and supplies, Lee surrenders at Appomattox Court House

Union soldiers under General William Tecumseh Sherman occupying a former Confederate munitions dump in Atlanta, September–November 1864

- Vastly better equipped in terms of manpower, resources, and industrialization, the North had the ability to last out a war.
- The North's blockade of the South further reduced the resources available to the Confederacy.
- Southern states were reluctant to supply men for different areas. Quoting the case of New Orleans – in 1862 5,000 men were hastily taken from New Orleans to reinforce a Confederate army in Tennessee. New Orleans promptly fell to the Union.
- Unlike earlier Northern commanders, Grant was bold. Determined to win at all costs, he absorbed losses but stayed in pursuit of Lee until Southern forces could continue no longer.

A soldier of the 33d New York Infantry

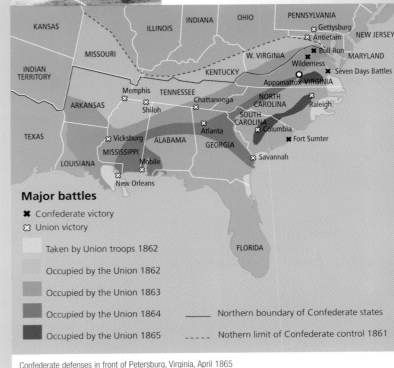

Major battles

✕ Confederate victory
⊗ Union victory

Taken by Union troops 1862
Occupied by the Union 1862
Occupied by the Union 1863
Occupied by the Union 1864
Occupied by the Union 1865

——— Northern boundary of Confederate states
- - - - Nothern limit of Confederate control 1861

Confederate defenses in front of Petersburg, Virginia, April 1865

THE NATURE OF THE WAR

The Civil War saw a military transition. Part of the war was conducted in a classical fashion: large armies maneuvered, faced each other, and charged. On the other hand, it was the first of the truly modern wars, with soldiers transported by railroad or steamship, and new military technologies used such as rifled weapons, giant cannon, torpedoes, and submarines. The Civil War also saw the first clash of ironclad ships, making wooden warships instantly obsolete.

The Boxer Rebellion

A response to China's troubles at the end of the 19th century, particularly the defeats by other countries, the Boxer Rebellion began as an uprising against the government. The rebels were persuaded to direct their anger towards foreigners. The easy defeat of the Boxers and Chinese government forces by foreign nations added to China's problems and contributed to the great upheaval of the revolution a decade later.

Boxer prisoners captured by the US 6th Cavalry in Tianjin

Firing from shelter, Chinese soldiers try to keep the foreign forces pinned down in Tianjin, 1900

THE BOXERS

Attacks on foreigners were led by a secret society called the Society of Righteousness Harmony. This was mistranslated as the Society of Righteous Fists, or Boxers. The misunderstanding was complicated by the fact that some Boxer martial artists believed that if they wore special shirts and trained in special ways, they would become invulnerable. The first Boxer slogan was "Overthrow the Qing and exterminate the foreigners". After some government officials supported them, the Boxers changed their slogan to "Uphold the Qing and exterminate the foreigners". Essentially a mob movement, the Boxers did not win the support of all layers of Chinese society.

CAUSES

• At first, the Boxers were rebelling against the unpopular and increasingly incompetent Qing dynasty (Manchus), as well as expressing hatred of foreigners. They were persuaded to direct all their resentments onto foreigners.

• General anti-foreign feelings deepened into anger at the humiliating treaties forced on China by Japan and European nations in the last 60 years through the Opium Wars and other defeats.

• Hatred of Christian missionaries, who had gained concessions such as immunity from Chinese law, and were pressing for changes in Chinese society.

• Resentment over criminals who escaped justice by claiming to be Christian converts, and sought immunity in foreign enclaves.

• Economic problems, caused partly by the unequal trading conditions forced on China, made ordinary people ready to riot.

CONSEQUENCES

• 230 foreigners were killed along with many thousands of Chinese Christians, civilians, soldiers, and Boxers.

• Total humiliation for China, who was forced to grant more concessions to foreigners.

• The Qing government accepted the need for reforms but in the end these simply destabilized the country further.

• Taxes were raised to pay for the war reparations.

• All of these contributed to the growth of revolutionary feelings and the eventual 1911 revolution. Many Chinese blamed the Qing for the defeat, and felt that the only way for China to progress and stand against foreign nations was to overthrow the existing regime.

CHINESE OFFICIALS

Empress Cixi (Tz'u-hsi), 1835–1908
The real ruler of China for many years. Conservative, and unable to make the rapid changes needed to adapt to the pressures of the western world. Favored limited change, but opposed political modernization. c. 1851 Enters the Forbidden City as a concubine of Qing emperor Xianfeng. 1856 Gives birth to the emperor's only son, Tongzhi. 1861 Upon the emperor's death stages a coup to become regent for her son. Is titled Empress Dowager. 1898 Places emperor Guangxu under house arrest and becomes regent again. Resolves to refuse further concessions to foreigners. 1900 Allows Boxers into Beijing.

Prince Tuan, ?–1909
Nephew of emperor Xianfeng. Married niece of Cixi. Believed that China's problems were caused by westerners diluting traditional values. Member of the Clan Council, of highest ranking Manchu nobles, advising the empress. 1898 Horrified by emperor Guangzu's attempted reforms (Hundred Days Reforms), and conspires against him. Supports Cixi coup against Guangzu. 1900 Receives Boxers in Beijing. Wants to integrate them into imperial structure. Persuades Cixi to let Boxers stay in Beijing and to use them against foreigners. 1901 Condemned to death in Boxer Protocol but sentence commuted to exile in Turkestan.

Yu Xian (Yu Hsien) ?–1901
Anti foreigners; wanted to use the Boxers to supplement imperial forces against western influence. 1896 Official in Shandong province when a group called "Big Swords" attacks Christians. Treats Big Swords leniently, interpreted by many as message that anti-foreign groups are accepted by government. 1899 His open support for Boxers helps reconcile the movement to Qing government. 1900 As Governor of Shanxi province, blamed for slaughter of missionaries there. 1901 Executed by foreign demand.

Yuan Shikai, 1859–1916
1898 Appointed commander of the modern New Army, trained to equal western forces. Nov 1899 Appointed governor of Shandong province where Boxer activity first emerges. Calls Boxers "criminals" but, on advice of Prince Tuan, does not suppress them. 1900 Sits on the fence, deliberately delaying imperial order to oppose foreigners, and persuades foreign nations that Cixi has been ill-advised in opposing them. 1912 Becomes president after 1911 revolution.

EXTRACT FROM GENERAL CHAFFEE'S REPORT, 1900

... At about 3 o'clock p.m. our advance had arrived opposite the legations ... Upon entering the legations the appearance ... showed every evidence of a confining siege. Barricades were built everywhere and of every sort of material, native brick being largely used for their construction, topped with sandbags made from every conceivable sort of cloth, from sheets and pillowcases to dress materials and brocaded curtains. Many of the legations were in ruins, and the English, Russian, and American, though standing and occupied, were filled with bullet holes from small arms, and often having larger apertures made by shell ...

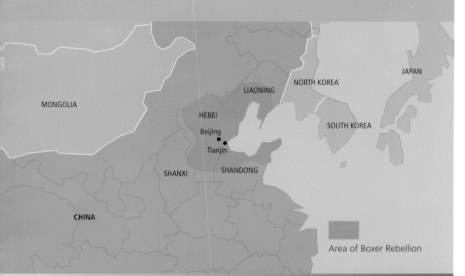

Area of Boxer Rebellion

KEY DATES

Nov 1899	Boxer groups in Shandong (Shantung) province begin attacks against Chinese Christians.
Dec	Christian missionaries and other foreigners are attacked. Western governments protest.
Jan 11, 1900	Empress Cixi responds that Boxers are not criminals, but part of normal Chinese society. Western nations send forces to China.
May 30	Ministers of the foreign legations in Beijing jointly request help from their fleets off the coast of Tianjin (Tientsin) in north China.
May 31 and Jun 4	Eight foreign nations (Austria, France, Germany, Italy, Japan, Russia, United Kingdom, and United States) agree an unprecedented alliance against the Boxers. A combined force of 431 foreign soldiers and sailors arrives in Beijing to protect the legations.
Jun 9	Boxers attack foreign property in Beijing.
Jun 11	Japanese legation official Sugiyama is killed.
Jun 17	An Allied force takes the strategic Taku Forts on the coast by Tianjin.
Jun 20	The German minister in Beijing is killed.
Jun 20–Aug 14	Boxers begin 55-day siege of the foreign legation quarter in Beijing. Foreigners band together for self-defense.
Jun 21	China declares war on the Allies.
Aug 4	The China Relief Expedition (20,000 strong, including 2,000 American sailors and soldiers) breaks out of Tianjin to head for Beijing. The foreigners are better armed and trained than Chinese armies.
Aug 5–6	Relief force wins battles of Pei Tang and Yang Tsun.
Aug 12	Relief force reaches Beijing. Battles with Chinese government forces and Boxers.
Aug 14	Legations successfully relieved. The victorious Allied army sacks the city.
Dec 22	Allied peace proposals put forward.
Jul 7, 1901	Peace Protocol of Beijing or Boxer Protocol signed.

CHINESE REPARATIONS

Under the peace agreement or Boxer Protocol of 1901, China had to accept many humiliating concessions. The Qing government agreed to execute or punish officials who were linked to the Boxers, to allow foreign troops in China, and to pay crippling war reparations of 450,000,000 tael of silver ($330 million US dollars) within 39 years. This amount was chosen as representing one tael per person, with the Chinese population estimated at 450 million. Interest was added, and by 1939 China had paid 668,661,220 taels. In order to help China modernize, America and Britain used some of the money for advanced education of Chinese students. Many of the students who benefited from this went on to take part in the Chinese revolution.

Captured rebels often faced immediate execution, as in this case in Tianjin, 1900

One of the gates keeping Chinese people out of the foreign legation quarter in Beijing

ALLIED COMMANDERS

Sir Claude Maxwell MacDonald, 1852–1915
British diplomat, originally trained as a soldier. **1900** As senior foreign minister in Beijing, he takes command of defense of legations. Helps Japanese and Europeans overcome traditional enmities to work together. Uses military experience to organize soldiers and civilians in defense. **1905** Appointed as first British ambassador to Japan.

General Adna Romanza Chaffee, 1842–1914
Commander of the American forces. **1861** Joins Union army during the Civil War. **1865–92** Fights in Indian Wars against rebellious Native Americans. **1898** Promoted to brigadier-general during Spanish-American War. **1900** Sent to China to command the China Relief Expedition of approximately 2,500 Americans. Plays major part in rapid Allied advance on Beijing and relief of the legations. **Aug 14, 1900** Condemns looting of Beijing after Allied victory. **Feb 1901** Promoted to major-general. **Jul 1901** Appointed military governor of the Philippines. **1904** Becomes chief of staff of the US army.

EXTRACT FROM THE BOXER PROTOCOL

Article II ... The following punishments on the principal authors of the attempts and of the crimes committed against the foreign Governments and their nationals ...

Article V China has agreed to prohibit the importation into its territory of arms and ammunition ...

Article VI ... His Majesty the Emperor of China agreed to pay the Powers an indemnity of 450,000,000 ... tael ...

Article VII ... the quarter occupied by the Legations shall be considered as one specially reserved for their use and placed under their exclusive control, in which Chinese shall not have the right to reside ...

Article VIII The Chinese Government has consented to raze the forts of Taku, and those which might impede free communication between Peking and the sea ...

Article XI The Chinese Government has agreed to negotiate the amendments deemed necessary by the foreign Governments to the Treaties of Commerce and Navigation and the other subjects concerning commercial relations ...

The Mexican Revolution

As the gap between the poor and the wealthy, land-owning classes in Mexico grew under the 30-year dictatorship of Porfirio Díaz, an effort to overthrow the dictator in 1910, led by Francisco I. Madero, grew into a country-wide revolt. Revolutionary leaders pursuing different goals fought for political control. The constitution introduced in 1917 made official some of the basic goals of the revolution, but fighting continued until 1920. Attempts to implement reforms took longer, and continue to this day.

April 1912: Sharpshooters could take advantage of the terrain and were indispensable in keeping government soldiers at bay

Revolutionary fighter supporting Pancho Villa

CAUSES

• The Díaz regime was strongly geared to developing Mexico's economy, at the expense of a growing gap between the rich and the poor.

• The old system of landed estates (*haciendas*) had taken communal land holdings away from the indigenous people of Mexico, a process that accelerated under Díaz's rule. Díaz's controversial land laws allowed more land to become concentrated into the hands of a small minority of private investors, including many foreign companies, causing resentment amongst the majority of Mexicans.

• The lower classes felt exploited by the wealthier classes and unrepresented by government. The younger generation wanted more say in government, but there were no opportunities to be involved. Revolutionary ideas spread quickly.

• Díaz overturned his promise to hold a democratic election at the end of his term of office in 1910 by imprisoning his opponent, Francisco I. Madero, who had won the support of the rural poor and urban workers. Díaz's behavior caused popular leaders to unite against him, including Emiliano Zapata and Pancho Villa.

CONSEQUENCES

• A prolonged period of anarchy as revolutionaries divided into different factions and fought for power. Eventually the constitutionalists triumphed over the radicals at the cost of many lives lost, including children recruited to fight for the revolution.

• Around 900,000 legal Mexican immigrants arrived in the US between 1910 and 1920, and many more illegal immigrants are thought to have sought refuge there.

• A new Mexican constitution in 1917 effectively swept away the old power elite, introducing universal male suffrage and updating systems of land tenure, education, and employment, including the right to form unions and to strike. Although three autonomous branches of government were specified (executive, legislature, and judiciary), in practice Mexico has developed a centralized system with strong presidential control at all levels of government.

• In 1934, President Lázaro Cárdenas made official policy the objectives of the revolution, and organized a major land redistribution effort, though industrialization was to take priority over reform soon after in response to an economic crisis.

CONSERVATIVES

Porfirio Díaz, 1830–1915
Dictator and president of Mexico from 1876, who pledged he would serve just one term as president. His modernization program was seen to favor US business and wealthy landowners, who were allowed to encroach onto village land. **1884** Re-elected after one term, ignoring his own "no re-election" slogan (he considered himself to be the best person to bring stability and development to Mexico). **1910** His electoral fraud leads to widespread anger and sparks the revolution. **May 25, 1911** Forced to hand over power to Madero.

Victoriano Huerta, 1854–1916
Mexican general who staged a coup d'état against Francisco I. Madero. President of Mexico (1913–14). **Oct 1911** Pledges allegiance to Madero after fall of Díaz. **Feb 1913** Proclaims himself president after Madero is forced from power. Establishes a harsh military regime. **July 14, 1914** Resigns and goes into exile. Dies of alcohol poisoning. Still reviled by modern-day Mexicans; nicknamed "El Chacal" ("The Jackal").

CONSTITUTIONALISTS

Francisco I. Madero, 1873–1913
Revolutionary leader and president of Mexico (1911–13). **1910** Jailed by Díaz to stop him winning the presidential election. **Nov 20, 1910** Calls for armed revolution against Díaz's regime and democratic reforms in the Plan of San Luis Potosí. **May 17, 1911** Signs Treaty of Ciudad Juárez demanding Díaz's resignation. **Oct 1, 1911** Elected president but his moderate policies fail to satisfy radical leaders, who revolt against his government. **Feb 18, 1913** Forced from power by the former dictator's nephew, Felix Díaz, and his general, Huerta, in a military coup. Executed four days later.

Venustiano Carranza, 1859–1920
Revolutionary leader and president of Mexico (1917–20). **1911** Supports Madero's presidency. **1913** With his "Constitutionalist Army" (named for his support of the reinstatement of the 1857 liberal constitution) he opposes Huerta. **1915** Assumes presidency but meets opposition from radicals. **1917** Elected president and issues new constitution. **1920** Murdered by rivals.

Mexican railroads and Mexico City became the focus of much of the fighting during the revolutionary wars. Following Madero's demise, Huerta's forces held the railroads and the main towns. Against them, Pancho Villa's supporters, located in the north, attacked from surrounding land. Emiliano Zapata's forces stayed close to Morelos, the state Zapata was most concerned to protect.

Revolutionary fighters in training at a rebel outpost, March 1911

--- Strategic railroads

■ Strongholds of revolutionary forces united against Huerta

PRELUDE TO 1910

In 1810, Mexico began its fight for independence from Spanish colonial rule. At the same time, a movement was growing supporting the dispossesed indigenous peoples of Mexico and calling for land redistribution, a transformation of society, and social justice. Led by Miguel Hidalgo, a popular rebellion against the Spanish government – a fight of poor against rich – was cruelly suppressed and Hidalgo executed. José María Morelos continued a guerrilla war but was caught and executed in 1815. Though independence was achieved in 1821, the state continued to favor the Roman Catholic Church and landowners. Mexico's social revolution had been contained, but temporarily.

Pancho Villa's artillery in Mexico City after the fall of Huerta, July 1914

RADICALS

Pancho Villa, 1878–1923
From a peasant family, he led guerrilla fighters in northern Mexico during the revolutionary war. His bandit life began aged 16 when he shot dead the son of a *hacienda* owner who had seduced and abandoned his sister. After time in jail, he joined the fight to redistribute wealth and defeat federal forces. **1911** Supports Madero in Battle of Juárez, defeating federal army of Díaz. **1913–14** Provisional governor of Chihuahua. **1913** Supports Carranza in overthrow of Huerta, but later denounces Carranza.

Emiliano Zapata, 1879–1919
Revolutionary hero whose legacy continues to this day (the revolutionary Zapatistas of Chiapas, begun in 1994, are named for him). Led revolutionary guerilla fighters ("Zapatistas") against Porfirio Díaz's regime, then against Constitutionalists, in support of land reform and relief of poverty for peasants in southern Mexico. **1910–11** Sides with Madero to defeat Díaz. **1913–19** Fights against Huerta, then against Carranza.

KEY DATES

1909	Emiliano Zapata recruits thousands of peasants to attack *haciendas* and reclaim their land.
Oct 1910	Porfirio Díaz re-elected president. Francisco I. Madero thrown into jail during the election to stop him winning.
Nov 20	Madero issues Plan of San Luis Potosí denouncing Díaz's presidency and calling for revolution.
1910–11	Insurgence spreads to south (led by Zapata) and north (led by Pancho Villa and Pascual Orozco). Díaz's administration crumbles as c. 17,000 people take up arms against the government.
May 10, 1911	Orozco and Villa capture the federal stronghold of Ciudad Juárez (northern Mexico). Díaz hands over power to Madero, who is elected president with an overwhelming majority and US support (takes office Nov 6, 1911).
Nov 25	Madero's delay in implementing land reforms frustrates Zapata, who issues Plan of Ayala, calling for return of lands to dispossessed poor and the implementation of liberties. Zapata wins mass support of rural poor.
Mar 25, 1912	Revolt led by Orozco in northern Mexico, who calls for agrarian reform in Plan of Chihuahua.
Feb 18, 1913	Madero's commander-in-chief, General Victoriano Huerta, stages a coup d'état (with support of US ambassador, Henry Lane Wilson), forcing Madero to resign; Madero is executed (Feb 22, 1913). Huerta assumes presidency without support of incoming US president, Woodrow Wilson.
Mar 25	Constitutionalist Venustiano Carranza denounces Huerta in Plan of Guadalupe, accusing him of restoring a dictatorship. He is supported by Villa, Zapata, Álvaro Obregón (president of Mexico 1920–24), and the US.
Jul 1914	Huerta flees; his forces surrender (Aug 14, 1914). Carranza assumes presidential authority (1915).
Nov	Villa and Zapata denounce Carranza for failing to implement widespread land reform, leading to civil war with many people killed in the fighting (around 200,000 from 1914–15). Carranza is forced out of Mexico City.
Oct 1915	US recognizes Carranza presidency after revolutionaries are driven from Mexico City.
Oct 1916	Constitutionalists create a new government and hold elections, which Zapata protests are non-representative.
1917	New Mexican constitution issued under Carranza.
Apr 9, 1919	Zapata murdered after Carranza puts bounty on his head.

The Chinese Revolution

Imperial China lasted more than 2,000 years. Dynasties came and went, but there was an underlying continuity of social structure and hierarchies. In less than 40 years this was overturned. A relatively peaceful revolution, then a series of internal conflicts, interrupted by a struggle against Japanese invaders which became part of World War II, culminated in the establishment of the communist People's Republic of China.

A typical scene in late 1960s China: ordinary people like these sailors meet to affirm their faith in Chairman Mao by quoting from his *Little Red Book*

CAUSES OF THE 1911 REVOLUTION

Failure of Government The Qing dynasty (Manchu) was in decline. Its government had become incompetent and corrupt. In addition, the Qing were powerless to prevent foreign countries imposing humiliating treaty terms on China and extending their influence in the country.

Nationalism As the Qing became more and more unpopular and inefficient there was a revival of old racial hatreds towards the Manchus, who had originally been foreign invaders.

Poverty Population growth had led to overcrowding and poverty in the countryside. High taxes – partly to pay for war reparations after the 1901 Boxer Rebellion – and corruption meant there were frequent uprisings in the late Qing period.

Progressive Ideas Progressives felt that traditional Confucian political ideas were holding China back. Foreign ideas of democracy and republicanism were filtering into China. Inflexible, based on a rigid hierarchy, Confucianism had been the cornerstone of Chinese society for centuries, so change would be truly revolutionary.

Revolutionary Organizations The revolutionary theorist Sun Yat-sen formed the first fully national group, the Revolutionary Alliance, in 1905. Its aim was to overthrow the Qing government, and it encouraged the growth of many other revolutionary groups.

The Late Qing Reforms (1901–11) China had been easily and soundly beaten by the foreign nations during the Boxer Rebellion. This humiliation forced the Qing to consider reforms. Paradoxically, these had the effect of hastening the revolution: constitutional changes did not give any powers to provincial leaders although imperial control over the provinces was weakening; the development of new, modern armies based in the provinces gave a military strength to the revolution; intellectuals sent abroad to study came back as revolutionaries.

CONSEQUENCES OF THE 1911 REVOLUTION

The revolutionaries of 1911 brought down the Qing dynasty but failed to replace it with strong national government. The first republican government, under Yuan Shikai, soon lost the support of many provinces. After his death in 1916 China experienced a complete breakdown in central government as it fell apart in "warlordism".

Note Chinese names are given here in modern Pinyin, with the older Wade-Giles system of transliteration in brackets. There are some exceptions: the names of Sun Yat-sen and Chiang Kai-shek are still spelt the old way in English; and the abbreviation KMT is still used even though the Kuomingtang in full is now spelt the Guomindang. Following Chinese custom, the surname appears first, followed by first names.

CAUSES OF THE 1927 CIVIL WAR

Failure of Government The revolutionaries were not able to establish strong, country-wide government. After the death of Yuan Shikai, China fell apart and the country was ravaged by competing warlords. Later, when the capitalist Guomindang (Kuomingtang or KMT) party emerged as ruling part of China, it did not exert control over all areas. It became so corrupt that it could not administer its own areas properly.

Communism With the failure of a parliamentary republic, liberals were willing to consider all alternatives, and many turned to communism.

Poverty China was so backward, rigidly hierarchical, and socially divided that, generation by generation, most families were becoming poorer. Change was urgently needed and many people thought the revolutionary Chinese Communist Party (CCP) was the only organization prepared to actually carry out reforms.

CONSEQUENCES OF THE CIVIL WAR

• The establishment of a dramatically different, communist society.

• As a communist regime in Asia, China had a huge effect on the Cold War. It supported other communist parties in Asia, became involved in the Korean War and the Vietnam War, and provided aid and arms to several third world countries.

• Some of Mao's policies proved disastrous, such as the Great Leap Forward which contributed to widespread famine. Other policies – purges, executions, work camps – were bloody and brutal.

• In the long-run a country with a predominantly peasant economy was transformed into an industrial superpower.

THE FIRST REVOLUTIONARIES

Sun Yat-sen, 1866–1925
The "father of the republic". **1895** Leads a failed revolution, forced to flee. **1905** With Huang Xing founds the Revolutionary Alliance. Develops his ideology of *Three Principles of the People*. **1911** Elected provisional president of the new republic. **1912** Allows army commander Yuan Shikai to be declared president. **1912** Forms KMT as a nationalist organization. **1913** Leads revolt against Yuan; forced to seek asylum in Japan. **1917** Returns to China to lead breakaway provinces.

Yuan Shikai, 1859–1916
Soldier and politician. **1898** Takes command of the modern New Army, trained to equal western forces. **1899–1901** Opposes Boxer Rebellion. **1908** Forced to retire. **1911** Called back by Qings to deal with revolution. Demands control of Peiyang Army. **1912** After revolution, becomes president of republic and assumes dictatorial powers. **1915** Declares himself emperor.

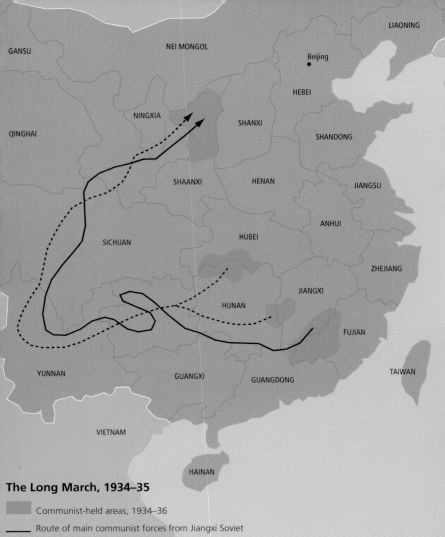

The Long March, 1934–35

- Communist-held areas, 1934–36
- —— Route of main communist forces from Jiangxi Soviet
- ‑‑‑‑ Route of communist forces from other communist areas

THE CULTURAL REVOLUTION

Together with Lin Biao, Mao urged young people to criticize anyone who he thought was undermining collectivism. He feared that the revolution was being betrayed. These "Red Guards" he unleashed in 1966 conducted a campaign of terror against everyone they accused of wrong thinking. Millions of people were killed or forced onto re-education or work farms. Children were encouraged to denounce their parents or teachers. The Red Guard created a personality cult around Mao, and their activities confirmed him as head of state. But, in 1968, he had to use the army to curb them.

Militia, or patriotic peasants, are trained to defend the People's Republic of China

COMMUNIST REVOLUTIONARIES

Mao Zedong (Tse-tung), 1893–1976
Communist theorist. Son of a reasonably well-off peasant farmer. Believed social revolution would come through peasants, not urban workers. **1921** One of the first members of CCP. **1934** Wants to disperse the Red Army from the Jiangxi Soviet and conduct guerrilla war. Overruled, the communists stay together, are surrounded, and have to break out on the Long March. **1935** During the Long March is appointed head of the CCP. **1949** Forms the People's Republic of China (PRC); becomes known as Chairman Mao. **1959** Steps down as chairman of PRC after failure of Great Leap Forward, but remains chairman of CCP.

Deng Xiaoping (Teng Hsiao-p'ing), 1904–97
Politician. **1924** Visits Soviet Union. **1929** Leads units against KMT. **1934** Veteran of Long March. **1954** Becomes secretary general of the CCP. **1966** Objects to excesses of Cultural Revolution and is "purged". **1973** Is "rehabilitated" and reinstated as deputy premier. **1980** Becomes premier; works at strengthening economy. **1989** Supports use of military force against Tiananmen Square pro-democracy demonstrators. Resigns.

Lin Biao (Lin Piao), 1908–71
Soldier. **1925–6** Trains at the KMT's important Whampoa (Huangpu) Military Academy; meets Zhou Enlai. **1928** Joins Jiangxi Soviet; develops Red Army's guerrilla tactics. **1945** Leads forces into Manchuria and forms the People's Liberation Army. Makes crucial decision to leave cities to KMT and concentrate on winning over surrounding countryside. **1968** Appointed Mao's successor. **1971** Killed in a plane crash, possibly while fleeing after political disputes.

Zhou Enlai (Chou En-lai), 1898–1976
Diplomat. **1915–23** Travels widely in Japan and Europe. **1927** Possibly captured by KMT but released because he had once saved Chiang Kai-shek's life. **1927–28** Visits Moscow; climbs to senior position in USSR-approved party hierarchy. **1931** Moves to Jiangxi Soviet. Becomes mediator of party disputes. **1949** Becomes premier of PRC. **1970s** Re-establishes relations with West.

Zhu De, 1886–1976
Soldier. **1911** Joins the revolution which overthrows emperor. **1922** Recovers from opium addiction. **1928** Joins forces with Mao, with whom he creates the Jiangxi Soviet, and develops successful guerrilla tactics. **1937** Becomes commander-in-chief of whole Red Army. **1949** Becomes vice-chairman of CCP.

NATIONALIST LEADERS

Chiang Kai-shek, 1887–1975
Soldier, politician. **1906** Joins army. **1911** Joins revolution. **1918** Joins Sun Yat-sen. **1924** Becomes head of Whampoa Military Academy. **1925** Takes over leadership of KMT. **1927** Attacks communists and declares his own national government. **Dec 1, 1927** Marries Soong Mae-ling, sister of Sun's widow, confirming his position as Sun's heir. **1940** Secures US support against Japanese and despite mutual hatred of US General Joseph Stilwell, becomes popular figure in USA. **1940s** Allows KMT to degenerate. **1949** Forced into exile in Taiwan, declares Republic of China there.

Madame Chiang Kai-shek, 1897–2003
Born Soong Mae-ling, younger sister of Sun Yat-sen's wife. Usually known as Madame Chiang. **1908–17** Educated in USA. **Dec 1, 1927** Marries Chiang Kai-shek. Takes roles in KMT government. **1943** Appears before US House and Senate, appealing for aid to KMT. Becomes huge hit in USA but is considered by communists to be decadent and corrupt. **1975** Returns to the USA after Chiang's death.

Zhang Xueliang (Chang Hsueh-liang), 1898–2001
Known as the "Young Marshal". Son of Manchurian warlord Zhang Zuolin (Chang Tso-lin). Dissolute drug addict. **1928** Japanese assassinate his father. He stops taking drugs, takes control of his father's forces, allies with KMT, and opposes Japanese. **1931** Forced to withdraw from Manchuria. **1936** Listens to CCP appeal for unity against Japanese, makes secret agreement with CCP, and forces Chiang to comply.

KEY DATES

REVOLUTION

Oct 10, 1911 Uprising in Wuhan army barracks occurs by accident: a small revolutionary group in the New Army accidentally lets off a bomb in the barracks. Fearing they will be arrested, they seize the arsenal and proclaim a revolution. Their general wins support from respectable merchants and gentry, and the governor of Wuhan immediately gives up.

Oct–Dec 15 other provinces (two-thirds of China) follow and declare independence from the Manchus. They are led not by revolutionaries but by local generals or gentry. The armies, based in the provinces, do not support the government.

Dec The breakaway provinces and members of Sun Yat-sen's Revolutionary Alliance meet in Nanjing and declare a new Republic of China. As a well-known revolutionary, Sun Yat-sen, abroad at the time, is elected provisional president.

1912 Hoping to arrange a peaceful transfer of power, Sun negotiates with prime minister Yuan Shikai, an ambitious and powerful general. Sun agrees to step down and allow Yuan to be president if he helps end the Qing government. Yuan accepts.

Feb 12 The boy emperor Puyi abdicates and the Qing government resigns. Puyi is allowed to live in the Forbidden City, Beijing.

Mar Yuan elected president of China.

1912 Sun Yat-sen and other Revolutionary Alliance members form the Nationalist Party (Kuomingtang/Guomindang or KMT) to oppose Yuan's growing powers.

1914 Yuan becomes dictator. Southern provinces, influenced by the KMT, begin to ignore him completely. He has little direct control over any of the provinces. Yuan plans to make himself emperor, but dies in 1916.

WARLORD PERIOD

1916 On Yuan's death the country falls into chaos with warlords taking local control. In general they oppress the peasants and fight amongst themselves. The KMT tries to form an alternative national government but is too weak. It controls just a small area in the south.

FIRST UNITED FRONT

1921 Chinese Communist Party (CCP) founded. Under pressure from Russia and with Russian financial aid (Russia wants to create a balance to countercheck Japan), CCP and KMT work together to try to bring order. Joint Northern Expedition to expand KMT control from south.

CIVIL WAR

1927 Now under right-winger Chiang Kai-shek, KMT turns on CCP, killing thousands. KMT declares a national government, with capital at Nanjing, and bans CCP. CCP revolts, e.g. in Shanghai, are defeated, survivors taking to the hills.

1928–31 Communists Mao Zedong and Zhu De win control of large rural area in southeast and name it the Jiangxi Soviet. They fight off four attacks.

1934 Chiang Kai-shek launches massive attack, encircling Jiangxi Soviet.

Oct 1934– Oct 1935 The Long March. 100,000 communists break out of Jiangxi Soviet and flee west then north, away from KMT areas. After the 6,000-mile (10,000-km) trek less than a third survive to find refuge in Shaanxi province.

JAPANESE INVASION AND SECOND UNITED FRONT

1931 Japan conquers Manchuria, establishes puppet state Manzhouguo (Manchukuo) under Puyi, the last Chinese emperor; begins incursions into China.

1936 CCP negotiates with generals attacking Shaanxi, calling for united front against Japanese. Generals agree, kidnap Chiang, and force him to comply.

Jul 1937 Formal alliance made as Japan launches full invasion.

Dec Japanese take Nanjing; KMT withdraws to southwest, followed by Japanese. CCP moves in behind Japanese lines.

1940 CCP controls vast area across north China, with capital at Yanan. CCP organizes peasants and conducts guerrilla war.

Dec 1942 USA enters World War II after Japanese attack on Pearl Harbor. USA gives war aid to China, which KMT hoards.

Aug Japan surrenders. CCP and KMT maneuver for cities, weapons, and provinces. CCP rushes north to Manchuria to grab Japanese equipment.

CIVIL WAR

Nov 1946 With communists winning support from peasants, KMT attacks.

Feb 1947 KMT pushes north, takes Yanan, but overstretches its line to Manchuria. CCP begins to surround KMT garrisons, cutting them off.

Nov 1948 CCP overwhelms KMT in Manchuria.

Nov 1948– Jan 1949 CCP overwhelms KMT in North China Plain.

Apr 1949 CCP moves into southern China.

1949 KMT defeated at Nanjing and retreats to Taiwan. Mao declares People's Republic of China (PRC).

The early days of the revolution in Hankou, Hubei: uncertain of the future, many people packed up their worldly goods and sought refuge from possible fighting

WHY THE COMMUNISTS WON

• The KMT had degenerated from a dynamic revolutionary nationalist group into corruption and incompetence. Its armies, although better equipped, were useless. Politically, it could not run basic government services in the areas under its control.

• Towards the end, KMT soldiers of all ranks were so disillusioned they often surrendered without a fight, or even joined the Red Army.

• The KMT lost the support of ordinary people when it did not take the initiative against the Japanese. Corruption, abuse of peasants, and brutal reprisals against suspected communists were all commonplace.

• The CCP became more popular than the KMT. It carried out land reforms in areas under its control, ensured that peasants were paid for supplies, and made efforts to win over ordinary people. The communists were respected for taking the initiative against Japan.

• After Chiang fled to Taiwan, most Chinese people welcomed the CCP because it provided strong, central government and offered the hope of peace.

Tired soldiers of the Red Army trek slowly through one of the many gruelling sections of the Long March, 1934–35

THE COMMUNIST SOCIAL REVOLUTION

Determined to destroy traditional hierarchies, the Chinese Communist Party declared war on landlords and forcibly redistributed land to peasants. Agricultural communities were collectivized, industry and businesses nationalized. In 1958 the Great Leap Forward was launched to accelerate economic growth – agricultural and industrial output was expected to increase dramatically through intensive work. New, disastrous farming methods were enforced, which, combined with bad weather, led to mass starvation.

Mao Zedong during the civil war

Mao Zedong followed by Lin Biao, holding a copy of *The Little Red Book*

EXTRACTS FROM QUOTATIONS FROM CHAIRMAN MAO (*THE LITTLE RED BOOK*), 1966

It is up to us to organize the people. As for the reactionaries in China, it is up to us to organize the people to overthrow them. Everything reactionary is the same; if you don't hit it, it won't fall. This is also like sweeping the floor; as a rule, where the broom does not reach, the dust will not vanish of itself.

Our duty is to hold ourselves responsible to the people. Every word, every act and every policy must conform to the people's interests, and if mistakes occur, they must be corrected – that is what being responsible to the people means.

Wherever there is struggle there is sacrifice, and death is a common occurrence. But we have the interests of the people and the sufferings of the great majority at heart, and when we die for the people it is a worthy death. Nevertheless, we should do our best to avoid unnecessary sacrifices.

It is only through the unity of the Communist Party that the unity of the whole class and the whole nation can be achieved, and it is only through the unity of the whole class and the whole nation that the enemy can be defeated and the national and democratic revolution accomplished.

Every comrade must be brought to understand that the supreme test of the words and deeds of a Communist is whether they conform with the highest interests and enjoy the support of the overwhelming majority of the people.

In order to build a great socialist society, it is of the utmost importance to arouse the broad masses of women to join in productive activity. Men and women must receive equal pay for equal work in production. Genuine equality between the sexes can only be realized in the process of the socialist transformation of society as a whole.

A group of Red Guards marching through villages during the Cultural Revolution, c. 1966

EXTRACT FROM SUN YAT-SEN'S *FUNDAMENTALS OF NATIONAL RECONSTRUCTION*, 1923

The principles which I have held in promoting the Chinese revolution were in some cases copied from our traditional ideals, in other cases modeled on European theory and experience and in still others formulated according to original and self-developed theories. They are described as follows:

I. Principle of Nationalism
… we should strive to maintain independence in the family of nations …

2. Principle of Democracy
All through my revolutionary career I have held the view that China must be made a republic …

3. Principle of Livelihood
… the principle of state ownership is most profound, reliable and practical …

To sum up, my revolutionary principles in a nutshell consist in the Three Principles of the People and the Five Power Constitution [executive, legislative, judicial, censorate, civil service system] …

The Russian Revolution

The Russian Revolution had a profound effect across the world, changing dramatically Russia's relations with the West, as well as the lives of its people. The consequences for Russia were enormous. It marked the end of the tsarist regime and the beginning of the communist Soviet Union. Democratic gains won were mostly disregarded by the dictatorship of Stalin that was to follow Lenin's death in 1924.

Lenin speaking at the 2nd Soviet Congress on October 26, 1917, the day after the storming of the Winter Palace; the meeting saw the establishment of a Bolshevik (communist) Soviet government, with Lenin as chairman

CAUSES

- Repressive tsarist regime, and a long period of unrest.

- Slow social change compared with the rest of Europe, where feudal restrictions were being eradicated and the state was becoming secularized, in particular in regions under control of the French Empire. In Russia, rural peasantry remained impoverished despite the 1861 emancipation of the serfs by Tsar Alexander II. The urban poor felt exploited in the newly industrialized centers.

- Huge losses sustained during World War I (1914–18) and the Russo-Japanese War (1904–05) were blamed on the tsar and weakened his position.

- Severe economic crisis with high food prices and food shortages spread discontent and encouraged revolt.

- Unrepresentative political system. The tsar's attempt to modernize political institutions by introducing a State Duma (legislative assembly) in 1906 failed to make the changes demanded by the growing intelligentsia.

- Development of revolutionary parties and ideas, in particular following "Bloody Sunday", named for the shooting of protestors by government troops that sparked the revolution of 1905.

- Personal limitations of the tsar: he lacked the qualities that may have averted the crisis. His wife was also unpopular.

CONSEQUENCES

- End of the tsarist regime and Russian Empire. Establishment of a new Russian republic.

- Social, political, and economic turmoil resulting in millions of lives lost through power struggles, civil war, assassinations, and state purges.

- Dramatic acceleration of Russia's modernization program introduced by Stalin's forced industrialization and collectivization, transforming a primarily agricultural state still influenced by feudalism into a superpower in 60 years.

- Challenge to western ideas of democracy and older economic, political, and social systems.

- Motivation for workers worldwide to unite and demand fairer rights.

- Impetus for colonies to fight for equal rights and freedom from colonial masters.

- Introduction of centralized, planned economies in many countries worldwide, following soviet-style economic planning.

- The communist dream of a worldwide revolution never materialized. Instead, the world's powers divided between communists (led by the Soviet Union) and anti-communists (led by the US). Support for communists served as a pretext for fascist parties, particularly in Germany, to draw recruits to attack the communists.

REVOLUTION IN 1905

The Russian revolution of 1905, a rebellion by the army, navy, and "commoners", arose out of discontent with the oppressive rule of the tsar and frustration at the slow realization of promised reforms. It was sparked by "Bloody Sunday", the killing and injuring of 1,000 or more people on a peaceful protest march outside the tsar's Winter Palace in St Petersburg, fired on by his own forces. Not a planned revolution, the revolt was a simultaneous protest by many different movements, from radical revolutionaries drawn from the educated elite to vast numbers of peasantry.

Demonstrators march to the Winter Palace, 1905

REVOLUTIONARIES

Vladimir Lenin, 1870–1924
Founder and leader of Bolsheviks (communists). Led the October 1917 Revolution and founded the Soviet state. Influenced by Karl Marx. **1895** Sets up Union for the Liberation of the Working Class. Arrested and exiled for three years. **1903** Instrumental in forming Bolshevik party. **1905** Takes control of revolutionary struggle. **1912** Controls Bolshevik publication *Pravda*. **1917** Leads October Revolution and elected head of Soviet state. **1924** Dies of a stroke.

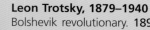

Leon Trotsky, 1879–1940
Bolshevik revolutionary. **1898** Arrested for anti-tsarist role in South Russian Workers' Union. Becomes member of Russian Social Democratic Labor Party. **1902** Escapes from exile in Siberia. **1917** Sides with Lenin in overthrow of Provisional Government. In the new Soviet government he becomes People's Commissar for Foreign Affairs. **1918** Becomes leader of Red Army (armed forces organized by Bolsheviks) and People's Commissar of War. **1920s** Following power struggle with Stalin, is expelled from Communist Party and deported from Soviet Union. **1940** Assassinated by a Soviet agent.

Joseph Stalin, 1879–1953
Bolshevik revolutionary. Leader of Soviet Union after Lenin. Rule characterized by political repression and mass terror. Adopted name "Stalin" aged 34, meaning "Man of Steel". **1902–17** Repeatedly arrested and exiled for political activities. **1912** Earns prominent role in Bolshevik party. **1917** Edits *Pravda* while Lenin in exile. **1922** Becomes general secretary of Soviet Communist Party. **1924** Lenin dies; Stalin defeats Trotsky in power struggle for leadership. **1928** Replaces New Economic Policy with collective farming and Five Year Plans. **1934–39** Eliminates political opposition and achieves absolute power in "Great Purge". **1953** Dies after a stroke.

Alexander Kerensky, 1881–1970
Moderate revolutionary instrumental in forcing abdication of tsar. **Feb 1917** Plays important role in February Revolution, leading to election as Minister of Justice, then Prime Minister in Provisional Government. Loses popularity when decides to continue Russia's involvement in World War I. **Oct 1917** Escapes Bolsheviks in October Revolution and lives in exile.

KEY DATES

Dates are based on the Julian calendar, which Russia used until 1918.

PRE-REVOLUTION

1894	Nicholas II becomes tsar.
1898	Russian Social Democratic Labor Party formed, from which the Bolsheviks (radical faction) emerges – later known as communists.
1900	Foundation of Socialist Revolutionary Party.
1903	Split between Bolsheviks and Mensheviks (moderates) at 2nd Congress of Russian Social Democratic Labor Party.
1904–5	Russia loses Russo-Japanese War.

1905 REVOLUTION

Jan 9, 1905	Dissatisfaction with Russian autocracy culminates in Bloody Sunday: unarmed protestors demanding social justice are shot at by tsar's troops. Strikes follow. Under pressure, the tsar introduces a "democratic" parliament (the State Duma), but it fails to represent the people.

1917 FEBRUARY REVOLUTION

Feb 1917	Strikers and protestors in Petrograd (St Petersburg) demanding "Bread", "Peace", and "Down with Autocracy" clash with tsar's forces. Leads to arrest of tsar's ministers (Feb 28), mutiny of government forces (Mar 1), and abdication of Tsar Nicholas II (Mar 2), who is later shot dead with his family (Jul 16, 1918).
Mar 3	Moderate socialists form a Provisional Government. Alexander Kerensky as prime minister begins an unpopular new offensive in World War I, which sparks the October Revolution.

1917 OCTOBER (BOLSHEVIK) REVOLUTION

Oct 2, 1917	Bolsheviks under Lenin promise "peace, land, and bread" and become the majority party.
Oct 25	Bolsheviks seize power from the unpopular Provisional Government by attacking the Winter Palace and taking key buildings in Petrograd.
Jul 10, 1918	A new Bolshevik government and constitution is adopted.

POST-REVOLUTION

1918–21	Rebellion against Bolshevik rule. All non-Bolshevik political activity is banned, including other socialist groups. "Enemies" of the revolution are executed or sent to labor camps.
1918–21	Civil war breaks out between radical (communist) revolutionaries ("Reds") and moderate socialists or Mensheviks ("Whites") and their foreign (capitalist) supporters. Communists win and establish the Union of Soviet Socialist Republics (Soviet Union) – dissolved 1991.
1919–21	Polish-Soviet War.
1921	Famine in Russia.
1921	Lenin replaces policy of War Communism with the New Economic Policy.
1924	Death of Lenin; Stalin takes over leadership after power struggle.

THE 1917 REVOLUTION

The political events commonly associated with revolution in Russia took place in 1917 and involved two parts: a February Revolution, which overthrew the last tsar of Russia, Nicholas II, replacing his autocratic rule with a hoped-for liberal republic. This was followed by the October Revolution of the same year, in which Lenin's Bolshevik party seized power from the Provisional Government, marking the beginning of communist rule, which was to spread to many countries during the 20th century.

Strikers and protestors, 1917

● Rural and urban areas most affected by revolution
✗ Main centers for distribution of Bolshevik propaganda
✗ Towns with active Bolshevik groups by 1917

ARCTIC OCEAN

Riga · Petrograd · Minsk · Kiev · Moscow · Karkov · Tula · Nizhniy Novgorod · Voronehz · Kazan · Perm · Yekaterinoslav · Samara · Ufa · Yekaterinburg · Rostov · Orenburg · Chelyabinsk · Omsk · Tiflis · Irkutsk · Baku · Vladivostok

RUSSIA

MONGOLIA

IRAN · CHINA

ROYALTY AND ASSOCIATES

Tsar Nicholas II, 1868–1918
Last tsar of Russia and staunch defender of autocracy. Unpopular, and incapable of solving Russia's economic and social crisis during World War I. **1894** Becomes tsar. **1904–05** Loses support after disastrous war with Japan. **1905** Following Bloody Sunday, agrees to a State Duma. **1906** Passes laws denying powers to Duma. **1914** Russian troops are unprepared for World War I. **1915** Departs for front line to inspire his troops, leaving government in the hands of his wife. Authority collapses. **Feb 1917** Forced to abdicate. **1918** Executed without trial by Bolshevik firing squad.

Tsarina Alexandra Feodorovna, wife of Tsar Nicholas II, 1872–1918
Born Princess Alix of Hesse (part of German Empire). Last tsarina of Russia. Unpopular and conservative. A genetic carrier of hemophilia, of which her son, Alexei, suffered. **1894** Marries Nicholas II. **1915** Tsar travels to front line, leaving Alexandra in charge. Relying on mystic Grigori Rasputin, she increasingly becomes the focus of negative rumors. **1918** Executed by firing squad by Bolsheviks.

Grigori Rasputin, 1872–1916
Spiritual healer from peasant family in Siberia. Notorious debauchee. Played a part in downfall of tsar. **1905** Tsarina's son, Alexei, appears to be aided by Rasputin's treatment of his condition. Rasputin gains the tsarina's trust and a position as a state official. **1915** Growing influence of Rasputin over tsarina while Nicholas II is at the front line during World War I brings disrepute to imperial family. **1916** Murdered by nobles anxious to protect Russian Empire.

Mikhail Rodzianko, 1859–1924
Loyal supporter of Nicholas II but favored democracy in Russia. A son of a wealthy landowner, he became a senior army officer, then leader of the 3rd Duma (1911). Critized Grigori Rasputin and warned the tsar of his growing influence. **1916** Tries to persuade Nicholas II to introduce reforms. **Feb 1917** Sends telegrams to tsar warning of discontent and approaching revolution. He urges the formation of a new government without delay. **Mar–Oct 1917** Supports Provisional Government but disapproves of Kerensky. Emigrates after Bolsheviks take control.

RUSSIA'S POLITICAL DIVISIONS

At the time of the 1917 revolution, Russians were divided into several political groups:

• Nobility and clergy supporting the old regime (the tsar's autocracy).
• Capitalists seeking a constitutional monarchy.
• The liberal ruling class seeking a constitutional democracy (to retain the monarchy but establish democratic parliamentary rule), the majority group in the Constitutional Democratic Party (formed 1905).
• Workers influenced by Marxism, represented in the Bolshevik and Menshevik sections of the Social Democratic Labor Party (created 1898). They believed the true revolutionaries were the urban workers, but aimed to unite workers and peasantry in a program of socialist revolution.
• Peasants and intelligentsia, members of the Socialist Revolutionary Party (formed 1902), who believed that Russia could transform from feudalism to socialism without the need for capitalism. They regarded peasants as the revolutionaries and prioritized abolishing private land ownership in favor of village communes and cooperative farming.

BOLSHEVIKS

Led by Lenin and strongly supported by urban workers, this radical faction formed following the 1903 split within the Russian Social Democratic Labor Party. Opposed to the moderate policies of the Mensheviks, in particular they rejected parliamentary government and wanted the proletariat (working class) to act immediately to take over control and land ownership.

MENSHEVIKS

Moderates, the Mensheviks urged less hasty change and included among their numbers many socialist intellectuals. Ultimately they wanted political power for the proletariat. Originally a Menshevik, Trotsky turned to support the Bolsheviks in 1917. The party was suppressed after the Civil War victory for the radicals.

First days of the October 1917 Revolution: an armed Russian soldier and two sailors on guard in Petrograd

How the Working People Can Be Saved From the Oppression of the Landowners and Capitalists Forever

"The enemies of the working people, the landowners and capitalists, say that the workers and peasants cannot live without them . . .

But this sort of talk by the landowners and capitalists will not confuse, intimidate, or deceive the workers and peasants . . .

To save the working people from the yoke of the landowners and capitalists forever, to save them from the restoration of their power, it is necessary to build up a great Red Army of Labor . . .

Labor discipline, enthusiasm for work, readiness for self-sacrifice, close alliance between the peasants and the workers – this is what will save the working people from the oppression of the landowners and capitalists for ever."

An Appeal to the Red Army

"Comrades, Red Army men! The capitalists of Britain, America, and France are waging war against Russia. They are taking revenge on the Soviet workers' and peasants' republic for having overthrown the power of the landowners and capitalists and thereby set an example to all the nations of the globe . . .

A few more months of fighting the enemy, and victory will be ours. The Red Army is strong because it is consciously and unitedly marching into battle for the peasants' land, for the rule of the workers and peasants, for Soviet power.

The Red Army is invincible because it has united millions of working peasants with the workers . .

The kulaks, the very rich peasants, are trying to foment revolts against Soviet power . . .

The middle peasants are not enemies but friends of the workers, friends of Soviet power . . . The middle peasants do not exploit the labor of others . . . as the kulaks do; the middle peasants work themselves, they live by their own labor. The Soviet government will crush the kulaks [and] pursue the policy of alliance between the workers and all the working peasants – both poor and middle peasants.

This alliance is growing all over the world. The revolution is drawing nigh, it is everywhere maturing . . .

Comrades, Red Army men! Be staunch, firm and united. March boldly forward against the enemy . . . The power of the landowners and the capitalists, broken in Russia, will be defeated throughout the world."

THE COMMUNIST MANIFESTO, 1848

Karl Marx, 1818–83

One of the world's most influential documents, written by communist theorists Karl Marx and Friedrich Engels, the Manifesto suggested a course of action for a proletarian revolution to overthrow the bourgeoisie and bring about a classless society. A product of the great changes that were happening in Europe before 1850, including the abolishment of feudal restrictions and secularization of the state in regions controlled by the French Empire, its core ideas were taken up and elaborated by Lenin. Lenin's theories served as a theoretical basis for the Bolshevik party and communism up until Stalin took control of the Soviet Union in 1924.

EXTRACT FROM THE COMMUNIST MANIFESTO

Preamble
A spectre is haunting Europe – the spectre of communism. All the powers of old Europe have entered into a holy alliance to exorcise this spectre: Pope and Tsar, Metternich, and Guizot, French Radicals, and German police-spies.

I Bourgeois and Proletarians
The history of all hitherto existing society is the history of class struggles.

Freeman and slave, patrician and plebeian, lord and serf, guild-master and journeyman, in a word, oppressor and oppressed, stood in constant opposition to one another, carried on an uninterrupted, now hidden, now open fight, a fight that each time ended either in a revolutionary reconstitution of society at large, or in the common ruin of the contending classes . . .

The bourgeoisie, wherever it has got the upper hand, has put an end to all feudal, patriarchal, idyllic relations. It . . . has left no other nexus between man and man than naked self-interest, than callous "cash payment" . . . It has resolved personal worth into exchange value, and in place of the numberless indefeasible chartered freedoms, has set up that single, unconscionable freedom – Free Trade . . .

The essential conditions for the existence and for the sway of the bourgeois class is the formation and augmentation of capital; the condition for capital is wage-labor. Wage-labor rests exclusively on competition between the laborers. The advance of industry, whose involuntary promoter is the bourgeoisie, replaces the isolation of the laborers, due to competition, by the revolutionary combination, due to association. The development of Modern Industry, therefore, cuts from under its feet the very foundation on which the bourgeoisie produces and appropriates products. What the bourgeoisie therefore produces, above all, are its own grave-diggers. Its fall and the victory of the proletariat are equally inevitable.

II Proletarians and Communists
. . . The Communists do not form a separate party opposed to the other working-class parties.

They have no interests separate and apart from those of the proletariat as a whole.

They do not set up any sectarian principles of their own, by which to shape and mold the proletarian movement.

The Communists are distinguished from the other working-class parties by this only: (1) In the national struggles of the proletarians of the different countries,

Leon Trotsky reviewing Red Army troops, 1918

THE RUSSIAN CIVIL WAR, 1918–21

LEADERS OF THE SOVIET UNION

Vladimir Lenin
Dec 30, 1922–Jan 21, 1924

Joseph Stalin
By end of 1920s–Mar 5, 1953

Georgy Malenkov
Mar 5, 1953–Sep 7, 1953

Nikita Khrushchev
Sep 7, 1953–Oct 14, 1964

Leonid Brezhnev
Oct 14, 1964–Nov 10, 1982

Yuri Andropov
Nov 12, 1982–Feb 9, 1984

Konstantin Chernenko
Feb 13, 1984–Mar 10, 1985

Mikhail Gorbachev
Mar 11, 1985–Dec 25, 1991

After the Bolsheviks seized power in 1917, their political opponents, including monarchists and foreign powers concerned to stop the spread of communism, joined forces to try and bring down the revolution. The civil war that followed, between the Bolsheviks ("Reds") and the anti-Bolsheviks ("Whites"), began with small forces and grew into a war on a massive scale, ravaging Russia over three years. The Whites lacked military coordination and effective political programs. The Reds, who were better disciplined and numerically superior, won the conflict and established the Soviet Union in 1922.

EVENTS

Jan 1918	Red Army created; after Leon Trotsky becomes War Commissar (April), it transforms from an undisciplined volunteer force to a rigorously disciplined regular army.
May 1918	Uprising of Czechoslovak Brigade: Czechs seeking independence from Russia clash with Red Army in Siberia. Joining forces with Whites, they capture Kazan in the east of Russia (under Alexander Kolchak).
Jan–Nov 1919	White Army advances from east (under Kolchak) and northwest (under Nikolai Ludenich), but Red Army (under Trotsky) forces them back. White advance from south (under Lavr Kornilov, then Anton Denikin), equipped with British tanks, poses greatest threat, but is driven back by Reds.
1920–21	Reds defeat remnants of White Army in Crimea (under Pyotr Wrangal) as Red forces swell following their return from fighting the Polish-Soviet War (1919–21). Communist rule is restored in Ukraine, Azerbaijan, Armenia, and Georgia.

Bolsheviks (Reds)	Anti-Bolsheviks (Whites)
5,400,000 troops (by 1921)	more than 1,000,000 troops
940,000 irrecoverable losses	more than 900,000 irrecoverable losses

White Army propaganda poster depicting Trotsky as a "Red devil"

Friedrich Engels, 1820–95

they point out and bring to the front the common interests of the entire proletariat, independently of all nationality. (2) In the various stages of development which the struggle of the working class against the bourgeoisie has to pass through, they always and everywhere represent the interests of the movement as a whole . . .

The communist revolution is the most radical rupture with traditional relations . . .

. . . The first step in the revolution by the working class is to raise the proletariat to the position of ruling class to win the battle of democracy.

The proletariat will use its political supremacy to wrest, by degree, all capital from the bourgeoisie, to centralize all instruments of production in the hands of the state, i.e., of the proletariat organized as the ruling class; and to increase the total productive forces as rapidly as possible.

Of course, in the beginning, this cannot be effected except by means of despotic inroads on the rights of property, and on the conditions of bourgeois production. . . In most advanced countries, the following will be pretty generally applicable: (1) Abolition of property in land . . . (2) A heavy progressive or graduated income tax. (3) Abolition of all rights of inheritance. (4) Confiscation of the property of all emigrants and rebels. (5) Centralization of credit in the banks of the state . . . (6) Centralization of the means of communication and transport in the hands of the state. (7) Extension of factories and instruments of production owned by the state . . . (8) Equal obligation of all to work . . . (9) Combination of agriculture with manufacturing industries . . . (10) Free education for all children . . .

When, in the course of development, class distinctions have disappeared, and all production has been concentrated in the hands of a vast association of the whole nation, the public power will lose its political character. Political power, properly so called, is merely the organized power of one class for oppressing another. If the proletariat during its contest with the bourgeoisie is compelled, by the force of circumstances, to organize itself as a class; if, by means of a revolution, it makes itself the ruling class, and, as such, sweeps away by force the old conditions of production, then it will, along with these conditions, have swept away the conditions for the existence of class antagonisms and of classes generally, and will thereby have abolished its own supremacy as a class . . .

III Socialist and Communist Literature
[This section highlights the differences between communism and other socialist doctrines of the time. Competing views are dismissed for advocating reform and failing to acknowledge the important role of the working class.]

IV Position of the Communists in Relation to the Various Existing Opposition Parties
[This section sets out the communist position on specific struggles going on in various countries at the time. It ends with a call to action:]

The Communists disdain to conceal their views and aims. They openly declare that their ends can be attained only by the forcible overthrow of all existing social conditions. Let the ruling classes tremble at a Communistic revolution. The proletarians have nothing to lose but their chains. They have a world to win.

Working Men of All Countries, Unite!

The Spanish Civil War

The Spanish Civil War began as a mutiny by conservative army officers against a liberal government. The insurgents were joined by the Catholic church, by aristocrats and monarchist groups, and by fascists. Republicans felt they were defending a democratically elected regime, and in many areas responded to the mutiny by behaving in a more extreme revolutionary manner – forming local militias, burning churches, overthrowing landlords, and declaring local autonomy.

Republican soldiers at the battle of Ebro, 1938: the Republican Army was practically destroyed in this pivotal battle

CAUSES

• Conservative army officers felt that the liberal government was destroying Spain's great traditions, particularly the strength of the army.

• The powerful Catholic church also felt threatened by the Republicans, who were making changes such as taking education away from the church.

• The landed aristocracy felt threatened by land reforms.

• An economic crisis, caused partly by the aristocracy moving huge amounts of money out of the country, led to strikes and a degree of chaos. The rightists began to feel that only they could restore order and greatness to Spain.

• On May 10, 1936 the conservative president Niceto Alcalá Zamora was replaced by the left-wing Manuel Azaña. Dissatisfied officers felt they had to act now before the country became more communist.

CONSEQUENCES

• The insurgents, known as "Nationalists", overthrew the Republican government and instituted a repressive, right-wing, fascist regime under General Franco as dictator.

• A country divided for many years as Franco deliberately followed a policy of revenge, executing or imprisoning thousands and oppressing former Republicans.

• The German Luftwaffe tested its new bombing theories in Spain, and gained experience of combined air and ground attacks. This would prove valuable to them in World War II.

Here we are, soldiers of a revolutionary army, defending Democracy against Fascism, fighting a war which is *about* something, and the detail of our lives is just as sordid and degrading as … in a bourgeois army.

George Orwell, volunteer in the International Brigades, (*Looking Back on the Spanish War*, 1943)

The Spanish Front in 1936

◉ Republican capital
○ Nationalist provisional capital
⊗ Major battles or bombings

Oviedo
Bilbao ⊗
Guernica ⊗
Burgos ○
FRANCE
SPAIN
Brunete ⊗
PORTUGAL
Madrid ◉
Barcelona ⊗
Tarragona
Teruel •
Valencia •
Badajoz ⊗
Seville
Granada ⊗
Tangier •
SPANISH MOROCCO

Republicans
Nationalists (Jul 1936)
Nationalists (Oct 1936)

REPUBLICAN LEADERS

Manuel Azaña, 1880–1940
Liberal lawyer; politician. **1931** Involved in revolution which led to King Alfonso XIII leaving Spain. **Oct 16, 1931–33** Prime minister before losing elections. **Jan 15, 1936** Achieves near-impossible by uniting squabbling left-wing parties in Popular Front coalition. **Feb 16, 1936** Wins elections, becomes prime minister. Oversees reforms that anger conservatives. **May 10, 1936** Becomes president. **Jul 1936** Does not want to fight a civil war but persuaded to stay in office. **Feb 5, 1939** Flees to France, where he dies.

Francisco Largo Caballero, 1869–1946
Left-wing socialist. **1931–33** Member of the Republican government. **Sep 1936** Becomes prime minister and concentrates on the war, putting social reforms aside. **May 1937** Argues with communists and is sacked by the president to appease communists. **1939** Escapes to France as the war ends. **1940** After Nazi invasion of France, captured, sent to Dachau Concentration Camp, but survives. Dies in Paris.

Juan Negrín, 1892–1956
Socialist; scientist. **1931** First elected to Cortes (parliament). **Sep 1936** Appointed minister of finance. Decides to transfer gold reserves to USSR in exchange for weapons. **May 17, 1937** Becomes prime minister. **Apr 1938** Also takes on ministry of defence. Appoints more and more communists to political and army posts, causing socialist and anarchist opposition. **1939** Flees to France. **1940** Flees to England after Nazi invasion of France.

La Pasionaria (Dolores Ibárruri), 1895–1989
Communist orator. Daughter of a miner, as a child lives in extreme poverty. **1920s** Writes for communist newspapers under the name *Pasionaria* (passion flower). **1930** Elected to Communist Party central committee. **1936** Elected to Cortes. **Jul 18, 1936** Coins Republican battle cry "No Pasarán!" ("They shall not pass!") during radio speech. **1939** Escapes to Soviet Union. **1977** Returns to Spain after Franco's death and is re-elected to Cortes.

1936

Feb 16	After years of political upheaval, Popular Front, a coalition of left-wing parties, wins general election and forms new Republican government.
Feb 28	Generals Francisco Franco, Emilio Mola, Juan Yagüe, and José Sanjurjo discuss opposition to government.
Jul 17	Military uprisings in Morocco and Seville.
Jul 20	General José Sanjurjo, nominal head of revolution, killed in plane crash. Insurgents fail to take Madrid and Barcelona, and appeal to Germany and Italy for help.
Jul 28	German aircraft transport Nationalist army from Morocco to Spain.
Aug 12	The first International Brigades volunteers reach Spain.
Aug 14	Nationalists take Badajoz and massacre about 4,000 Republicans.
Sep 27	Nationalists take Toledo.
Oct 1	Franco named Generalissimo; becomes supreme head of Nationalist government and armies.
Nov 6	Nationalist forces begin siege of Madrid.
Dec 22	Volunteers from Italy arrive in Spain to fight for the Nationalists.

1937

Feb 12	The International Brigades halt Nationalist advance at Jarama.
Mar 30	Nationalists advance to Basque region.
Apr 26	German planes bomb the Basque capital Guernica and strafe fleeing civilians.
Summer	More Nationalist victories.
Oct 1	Republican forces capture Belchite.
Oct 19	All of northern Spain in Nationalist control.
Dec 8	Nationalists begin bombing of Barcelona.
Dec 14	Republican offensive launched at Aragon.

1938

Jan 9	Republican Army captures the city of Teruel from the Nationalists.
Feb 22	Nationalist Army recaptures Teruel.
Apr 15	Nationalists break through to Mediterranean at Vinaroz, splitting Republican Spain in two.
Jul 25	Republicans go on the offensive, crossing the River Ebro.
Oct 4	International Brigades withdrawn from frontline and start to leave Spain.
Nov 16	Republicans defeated at River Ebro and retreat.
Dec 23	Nationalists begin offensive in Catalonia.

1939

Jan 26	Nationalists take Barcelona.
Mar 27	Nationalist Army enters Madrid after a siege of nearly three years.
Mar 30	Nationalist Army captures Valencia.
Apr 1	Franco announces end of the war.

The Republican infantry on the Aragon front, Dec 1937

WHY THE NATIONALISTS WON

Military Experience Although about half of Spain's soldiers supported the Republican government, nearly all the army's officers joined the Nationalists, giving them the benefit of military training and experience.

Foreign Support The Nationalists were supported by Germany and Italy. These two fascist governments not only supplied weapons to the Nationalists, but sent experienced military help – 80,000 Italian soldiers and thousands of German flyers from the Luftwaffe. This foreign intervention was crucial in the early months of the war when the first rebellion seemed in danger of fizzing out. Without German transport from Morocco, Franco and his experienced Army of Africa would not have reached Spain in time to turn the tide. Portugal also helped the Nationalists. Britain and France, however, when appealed to by the Spanish government, agreed a non-intervention pact. The USSR sent tanks and observers and offered moral support, but the real practical help the Republic received was from volunteers. About 40,000 men and women from around the world flocked to join the International Brigades. Few of these were trained soldiers and, often, they were not well armed.

Internal Dissent The Republicans were a collection of different left-wing and liberal groups, with differing motives and policies, including anarchists, Basque and Catalan separatist groups, socialists, and communists. The government was shuffled round several times because of political infighting. On the military front, socialist groups were suspicious of the communist-led International Brigades, and the anarchists formed their own brigades and did not want to follow the orders of the Republican Army. In May 1937 there was open fighting between different groups in Barcelona. Separatist groups were more interested in their own causes than in national unity. On the other hand, nationalist and fascist groups had more in common, and did not fight amongst themselves.

NATIONALIST LEADERS

Francisco Franco, 1892–1975
Soldier. **1920** Gains reputation for ruthlessness with Spanish Foreign Legion in Morocco. **1926** Becomes Europe's youngest general. **Oct 1934** Under right-wing government, suppresses miners' strike in Asturias. **1935** Appointed chief of staff, rids army command of left-wingers. **1936** Demoted by left-wing government. **Jul 1936** After initial hesitation, commits himself to revolt. **Sep 1936** Appointed commander of Nationalists. **1939** Becomes authoritarian dictator propped up by army and Catholic church.

Emilio Mola, 1887–1937
Soldier. **1927** Becomes brigadier-general. **1930** Becomes director of general security. **1936** Directs conspiracy with other officers against Republican government. Turns down compromise offer of position of minister of war in government. **Jul 19, 1936** Declares revolution. **Sep 1936** Takes control of Nationalist Army of the North under Franco's supreme command. **Jun 3, 1937** Killed in plane crash.

José Antonio Primo de Rivera, 1903–36
Lawyer; son of Miguel Primo de Rivera, military dictator, 1923–30. **1933** Sets up fascist party, Falange Española which becomes dominant political force amongst Nationalists. **Feb 1936** Badly defeated at elections, but thereafter wins more support from the right when he criticizes Popular Front government. **Jul 1936** Captured in general round-up of right-wingers when relations deteriorate. **Nov 20, 1936** Executed by firing squad at insistence of anarchists.

Juan Yagüe, 1891–1952
Soldier. **1934** Serves with Franco in suppression of miners in Asturias. Joins the fascists. **1936** Joins Mola's military conspiracy. **Aug 1936** Gains nickname "Butcher of Badajoz" after massacring Republicans and encouraging mass rapes in Badajoz. Goes on to lead other important campaigns, contributing to Nationalist victory. **1939** Becomes minister of air in Franco's government.

The Cuban Revolution

Against all the odds, a tiny band of revolutionaries led a successful popular uprising that overthrew a repressive dictator, Fulgencio Batista. The revolution resulted in a communist state in anti-communist America's very backyard.

Fidel Castro during the guerrilla war in the Sierra Maestra, 1956–58; with his beard, habitual cigar, and olive green army fatigues, Castro became a familiar figure around the world

Flag of the 26th of July Movement, Castro's revolutionary group in 1955

CAUSES

Political Repression The corrupt, authoritarian government became even more repressive as it put down all protest movements.

American Imperialism There was a growing resentment in Cuba over US interference and support for the dictator Fulgencio Batista. The fact that foreign, usually American, businesses owned huge amounts of land was also a cause for resentment.

Social Inequalities The wealthy lived in luxury while their workers, particularly agricultural laborers, were so poor they were often malnourished.

CONSEQUENCES

• A communist state only 90 miles (150 km) from the USA created Cold War tensions which very nearly led to nuclear war between the USA and the USSR.

• Cuba fomented revolutions in other Latin American countries.

• After foreign businesses were nationalized, the USA imposed a full trade embargo against Cuba.

• Social changes gave education, health care, and employment to all Cubans, but an economic depression, caused partly by a US embargo, kept the country poor.

THE SOCIAL AND ECONOMIC REVOLUTION

• "In the interests of the Cuban people" foreign-owned businesses were nationalized.

• A quarter of land was seized from rich landowners and redistributed to the poorest peasants.

• Volunteers taught peasants to read and write.

• Free schools and health services were set up and full employment provided.

• Public religious worship was banned.

• Racial discrimination was banned.

• Independent newspapers were banned.

• Castro ruthlessly executed many of Batista's supporters, particularly those who had tortured revolutionaries, and arrested or expelled influential political rivals.

• In 1961 Cuba turned to the communist world for support and officially became communist.

REVOLUTIONARY LEADERS

Fidel Castro, Aug 13, 1926–
Prime minister, then President of Cuba (1959–). **1939** Aware as a child of huge inequalities, organizes his father's workers into a strike. **1945** Studies law. **1947** Joins radical new political party, Cuban People's Party, and takes part in revolutionary activities in Dominican Republic and Colombia. **Jul 26, 1953** Leads failed assault on Moncada barracks. **Nov 25, 1956** Leads 82 activists from Mexico and begins guerrilla war, winning over the population. **Feb 1959** Victorious, begins social and economic revolution. **2006** Health begins to fade.

Ernesto "Che" Guevara, 1928–67
Argentinean revolutionary icon. Disgusted by corruption and social inequalities, becomes Marxist while still in his teens. **1954** Takes part in failed revolution in Guatemala. **1954** Flees to Mexico. Meets Castro. **1956** Joins *Granma* expedition to Cuba. **Dec 1958** Defeats government forces in decisive battle at Santa Clara. **1965** Goes to Africa to support communist revolts. **1967** Tries to organize revolution in Bolivia, is captured and shot.

Raul Castro, 1931–
Fidel's youngest brother. **1953** Takes part in Moncada assault, is jailed. **1956** Takes part in expedition from Mexico, becomes guerrilla leader. **1959** Appointed armed forces minister, thereafter takes many other government posts, including position of "heir to the throne". Is thought to be the world's longest serving defense minister. Close confidante of Fidel. **2006** Takes over temporarily during Fidel's illness.

Celia Sanchez, 1920–80
1950s Joins revolutionary movement after discovering abuses of Batista's government. **1957–59** Already an armed rebel, meets Castro in the Sierra Maestra, becomes Castro's lover. Fights as a guerrilla and also becomes one of the revolution's most successful messengers, moving unsuspected between mountains and towns. **1959** Becomes secretary to the presidency. Acts as Castro's assistant, has enormous influence on him. Concerned with social reforms and women's rights. **1980** Dies from cancer.

KEY DATES

Jul 26, 1953 Fidel Castro leads 160 young revolutionaries in an assault on the Moncada army barracks in Santiago. He hopes to inspire a popular uprising, but half his men are killed, most after torture, and he and the other survivors are imprisoned. At his trial Castro says "History will absolve me".

1955 Castro released after Batista feels confident of his political control. Forms new revolutionary group named for the day of the Moncada assault, the 26th of July Movement. For his own safety, Castro goes into exile in Mexico and trains a small guerrilla army, including Che Guevara.

Dec 2, 1956 Sailing from Mexico on the *Granma*, Castro and his 82 men arrive in Cuba to raise a revolution. In another disaster, the army is forewarned, back-up fails to arrive, and most of the revolutionaries are killed. The survivors are rescued and regroup in the Sierra Maestra mountains, eastern Cuba, and launch a guerrilla war.

1957 Castro makes one of his first propaganda coups when he convinces a *New York Times* journalist that he has a huge, popular army. The news is widely reported, frightening Batista but encouraging other rebels. He begins to win support from peasants and towns. Members of 26th of July Movement in cities start urban revolts and other rebel groups begin spontaneous uprisings.

1958 Rebels set up a radio station, announcing their proposed reforms and giving news of the revolution.

May 24 Brutally treating suspected rebels, Batista invades the Sierra Maestra with tanks, planes, and a large force. The outnumbered rebels repulse the attack, and continue to beat much larger forces, taking town after town.

Sep Castro goes on the offensive, sending two columns, under Che Guevara and Camilo Cienfuegos, to cut the island in two and advance on Havana. His own and his brother's forces advance on Santiago.

Dec 31 In the last major battle of the revolution, Santa Clara is captured by Guevara and Cienfuegos, who then move almost unopposed to Havana.

Jan 1, 1959 Batista gives up and flees with a $300 million fortune.

Jan 2 Castro enters Santiago.

Jan 6 Castro arrives in Havana and takes over the country. During his first speech as ruler, a white dove lands on his shoulder, taken by many to be a positive omen.

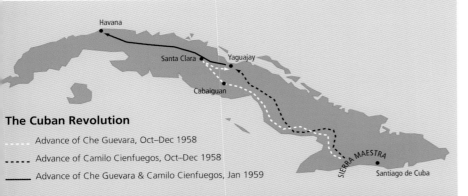

The Cuban Revolution

- - - - Advance of Che Guevara, Oct–Dec 1958
- - - - - Advance of Camilo Cienfuegos, Oct–Dec 1958
───── Advance of Che Guevara & Camilo Cienfuegos, Jan 1959

GOVERNMENT FIGURES

Fulgencio Batista, 1901–73
Ruler of Cuba (1934–44, 1952–59) **1921** Joins Cuban army. **1933** Leads army coup ("Revolt of the Sergeants"). **1934** Deposes president and becomes *de facto* ruler until – with a short gap – 1944. Wins US support and becomes friend of American gangster Meyer Lansky. Takes money from Mafia who begin to build casinos and hotels in Cuba and control drug traffic. **1952** Leads another revolt, takes over, suspends constitution. Opens up Cuba even more to American businesses. Runs corrupt, repressive regime. **Jan 1, 1959** Flees Cuba, dies in Portugal.

Colonel Esteban Ventura, 1913–2001
1930s Joins police force. Widely hated and notorious for torturing and killing suspects. **1957–58** During revolution makes no attempt to hide murders, shooting suspects in public or dumping tortured bodies in the streets. **Jan 1, 1959** Flees with Batista, finds refuge in USA. Sets up private security firm. Despite appeals for extradition to face trial, dies in USA.

ASSASSINATION PLOTS AGAINST CASTRO

Castro claims to have survived 450 murder plots. At least 30 plans for his assassination are known, most instigated by the CIA, sometimes with the assistance of the Mafia. The plots include:
- exploding cigars
- poisoned cigars
- a diving suit impregnated with tuberculosis bacteria (Castro was a keen diver)
- an exploding seashell
- a booby-trapped fountain pen
- dusting the insides of his shoes with a chemical aimed at making his beard (symbol of virility and power) fall out

THE BAY OF PIGS

On April 16, 1961 Cuban exiles who had been trained by the CIA in America landed at the Bay of Pigs on the south coast of Cuba with the aim of overthrowing Castro. Although the invasion was funded and equipped by the USA, President Kennedy did not let US forces openly take part for fear that it might escalate Cold War tensions and lead to war with the USSR. The expedition was a complete fiasco. Cuban jets sank the invading boats, and shot down their supply planes. The invaders were captured and to humiliate America even further, Castro ransomed the captives for $50 million of equipment.

Fidel Castro at a meeting of the United Nations General Assembly, 1960

THE CUBAN MISSILE CRISIS

In June 1962 the USSR sent to Cuba nuclear missiles that could be aimed at and reach the USA. In November President Kennedy sent US warships to surround Cuba, intercept Russian ships, and search them for nuclear missiles. He then issued an ultimatum, threatening to invade Cuba if the USSR did not remove the missiles. The USSR swore to defend Cuba, and for days the world stood on the brink of nuclear war. The USSR basically backed down, and the two superpowers reached an agreement without involving Castro. The US promised not to invade; the USSR agreed to take away the missiles. Castro was furious because he thought he could have secured more concessions from the USA.

President Kennedy authorizes a naval blockade of Cuba, 1962

United States Department of Defense photograph of one of the launch sites for the Russian missiles, San Cristobal, Cuba

TRACKED PRIME MO

MISSILE SHELTER TENTS

MISSILE TRANSPORTERS

The Algerian War of Independence

France's occupation of Algeria began in 1830, with the excuse of stopping pirates from operating along the Algerian coast. The country was declared a French colony in 1834, and in 1848 it became an integral part of France. Native Algerians, however, were not considered full French citizens, but only French subjects. Their struggle for self-determination led to a savage conflict where terrorism was countered with more terrorism.

The Algerian Army of Liberation parading along the Boulevard Carnot, Algiers, July 1962

Algerian War of Independence

☒ Centers of the guerrilla attacks on November 1, 1954

Principal area of the revolution

CAUSES

• French colonial rule of Algeria was brutal and repressive.

• The French policy of "divide and rule" created a small, well-educated elite, whom the French intended to be the native bureaucrats. When these were still treated as second-class, they developed into the nucleus of the liberation movement.

• French colonists (*colons*) in Algeria, together with right-wing elements in France, refused to grant even the smallest concession.

CONSEQUENCES

• About 1 million Algerians were killed, along with about 25,000 French soldiers and colonists.

• The FLN tactics and ideals inspired other revolutionary or nationalist movements around the world, e.g. the African American civil rights movement.

• Algeria won independence but the nation was divided. The new government clashed with democratic, socialist, or Islamic movements. Ultimately the government became corrupt and incompetent, driving people to the only opposition, the independent mosques.

• The unstable Fourth Republic in France collapsed. General Charles de Gaulle returned to power, and the Fifth Republic, with strong executive powers, was created.

• France granted independence to other colonies smoothly and peacefully, avoiding further conflicts.

KEY DATES

Nov 1, 1954 The separatist organization National Liberation Front (*Front de Libération Nationale* or FLN), run from exile by Ahmed Ben Bella and eight others, launches surprise guerrilla attacks on army bases, police stations, and the French infrastructure. French forces respond with mass arrests of suspects, but at first use limited force against civilians.

Aug 1955 First FLN attack on civilians, massacring 123 people at the town of Philippeville.

1956 French forces begin harsher measures – the detention and relocation of whole village populations.

Jun FLN calls for reprisals.

Sep 30 France strengthens its defenses of military targets. Guerrillas start terrorist attacks on civilian targets. Terrorist attacks are also carried out in France, and opposing Algerian factions launch so-called "café wars" in France.

May 1958 With France under international pressure to end the war, the army and the right-wing fear Algeria will be abandoned. They attempt a military coup, calling for the return of war hero General Charles de Gaulle. The government collapses, and de Gaulle comes out of retirement to head a new Fifth Republic.

Dec 1960 *Colons* and army officers form the Secret Army Organization to carry out terrorist attacks on Muslims and pro-independence groups. It kills about 3,000 civilians, inspiring more reprisals.

May 1961 De Gaulle begins secret negotiations at Evian with FLN.

Oct 17 Police fire upon Muslim demonstrators in Paris. At least 70 people are killed.

Mar 19, 1962 Ceasefire. De Gaulle announces results of negotiations – a referendum for all Algerians on the future of their country.

Jul Referendum. Algerians choose independence.

1963 By now most French – about 1.4 million *colons* – and up to 100,000 Muslims have left Algeria.

KEY PERSONALITIES

Ahmed Ben Bella, 1918–
1947 Supports plans for armed revolution. Mar 1954 Becomes one of the nine "historic chiefs" of the war of national liberation. Oct 22, 1956 Captured and imprisoned by French. Mar 1962 Freed following ceasefire. Sep 15, 1963 Elected first president of the Algerian republic. Jun 19, 1965 Ousted by Boumédiène's military coup and kept under arrest until 1980.

Ferhat Abbas, 1899–1985
A moderate, originally supporting assimilation. Feb 1943 Issues a Manifesto of the Algerian People, calling for independence. 1946 Begins political career. May 1955 Joins FLN. 1958–61 Appointed president of the provisional Algerian government in exile. 1962 Supports Ben Bella and becomes president of the first Algerian Constituent Assembly, but resigns in 1963.

Houari Boumédiène, 1932–78
Soldier in the FLN army. Feb 1960 Becomes head of army general staff. May 1962 Leads army to take control of FLN after disagreements with civilian leaders. Jun 1962 Leads army to Algiers to impose Ben Bella as head of government. Jun 18–19, 1965 Worried that army is losing influence, leads military coup; becomes president until his death.

Charles de Gaulle, 1890–1970
Professional soldier, war hero who led the Free French forces during World War II. A right-winger but also a committed republican and pragmatist. Nov 13, 1945 Elected head of government, resigns on Jan 20, 1946. 1953 Retires from politics until called back as president in 1958. Apr 1969 Retires again.

The Cambodian Civil War

Although this was an internal civil war, it was complicated by the wider regional conflict, the Second Indochina War, or Vietnam War (1960–75). Two of the combatants there – communist North Vietnam and America – widened their struggle into Cambodia. With the foreign countries giving aid or support to opposing Cambodian sides, the civil war intensified. Peace only really returned to Cambodia when all foreign involvement ended.

Young Khmer Rouge fighters

CAUSES

• An emerging communist movement in Cambodia – the Khmer Rouge – was prepared for armed revolution.

• Lon Nol's 1970 coup which overthrew the monarchy (Prince Sihanouk) split the country, as royalists joined the rebel forces.

• Cambodians divided according to their feelings towards the various foreign countries who were fighting in Cambodia or supporting different sides. Pro-Westerners supported the US-backed Lon Nol government; many people were infuriated by US attacks which were aimed at North Vietnamese bases but killed thousands of Cambodians, so began to support the opposition to Lon Nol; others sided automatically with the Asian China/North Vietnamese-backed rebels.

CONSEQUENCES

• The establishment of the communist Khmer Rouge regime (Democratic Kampuchea), under Pol Pot, who killed about 2 million Cambodians through executions, starvation, and forced labor.

• About 6 million landmines were used, leaving thousands of Cambodians with an amputation injury.

• Although the communists won the war, there was no lasting peace. Resistance groups, variously backed by America, China, or Vietnam, fought against the Khmer Rouge, and, when it fell in 1979, against all later governments. It took international peace-keepers and the withdrawal of foreign influences to bring an end to fighting in the 1990s.

THE AFTERMATH

• Pol Pot killed everyone associated with the former government, even teachers and doctors. He set about creating a worker-peasant state. Cities were emptied and their populations forced into work camps in the countryside. He caused widespread famine by exporting food.

• Pol Pot turned on Vietnam, starting a war, but fell to a Vietnamese invasion in 1979. He then led guerrilla attacks, allied once more with Sihanouk. Vietnam withdrew, leaving a pro-Vietnamese government, in 1989.

• The United Nations arranged a peace treaty in 1991, followed by free elections, but the Khmer Rouge continued guerrilla attacks until it fell apart a year after Pol Pot's death in 1998.

THAILAND
LAOS
CAMBODIA
Phnom Penh
VIETNAM

Khmer Rouge "Killing Fields"
Approximate areas of main mass burial sites

KEY DATES

1968	Led by Pol Pot, Khmer Rouge begins armed insurrection.
1969	USA bombs North Vietnamese bases and Ho Chi Minh supply trail in eastern Cambodia.
1970	Prime minister Lon Nol leads a coup while Prince Sihanouk is abroad. He declares a republic, and orders Vietnamese out of Cambodia. He gets American aid and allows American raids on Vietnamese bases. Sihanouk arranges a coalition, including Khmer Rouge, against Lon Nol. China and North Vietnam give aid to Khmer Rouge.
1973	Pol Pot refuses to take part in an American-Vietnamese ceasefire. The US bombs east Cambodia.
1974	Rebels close in on the capital, Phnom Penh.
Apr 1, 1975	Lon Nol flees.
Apr 12	American embassy staff evacuate by helicopter.
Apr 17	Khmer Rouge enters Phnom Penh and begins its reign of terror.
Sep 9	Sihanouk becomes head of state, but is a figurehead only.

THE REVOLUTIONARY

Pol Pot c. 1928–98
A ruthless dictator. **1949** Becomes a communist while studying in France. **1962** After a government crack-down leads communist activists into hiding. **1968** Commands guerrilla uprising. **1970** Oversees secretive take-over of rebel coalition. **1976** Becomes prime minister of the new communist government and enforces disastrous, murderous policies to create a peasant society. **1979** Flees into hiding after Vietnamese invasion, conducts guerrilla warfare against new government. **1998** Dies under mysterious circumstances.

IN THE MIDDLE

Norodom Sihanouk, 1922–
At various times king, prince, president, and prime minister of Cambodia. **Nov 9, 1953** Upon Cambodian independence from France, becomes effective ruler. **1961** During Vietnam War tries to stay neutral, but permits North Vietnamese bases in Cambodia. Tries to keep balance between right and left in politics. Ends up pleasing no one. **Mar 18, 1970** Deposed by Lon Nol, so links with Khmer Rouge. **Apr 1975** Is symbolic head of Khmer Rouge government but retires to house arrest in 1976. **1993** Becomes king once more. **Oct 7, 2004** Abdicates due to ill health.

THE CONSERVATIVE

Lon Nol, 1913–85
Pro-American, right-wing civil servant and politician. **1966** First becomes prime minister. **1967** Violently suppresses peasant unrest over rice taxes, considered by some to be the real first act of the civil war. His repressive policies drive many peasants to support the Khmer Rouge. **1970** Overthrows Sihanouk. Introduces a pro-American regime, allowing American bombing in Cambodia. Fails to control widespread corruption in his government, and increasingly turns to clairvoyants for guidance. **Apr 1, 1975** Flees to the USA.

The Iranian Revolution

There were two separate phases of the Iranian Revolution. In the first, socialists, liberals, and Islamic religious groups united in a pro-democracy movement to overthrow the shah (king). The second phase, often called the Islamic Revolution, saw fundamentalist religious groups take power and create an Islamic republic.

Soldiers joining popular protests in 1979: the defection of large sections of the army made the shah's downfall inevitable

CAUSES

• The shah was dictatorial, authoritarian, and deeply unpopular. He allowed a brutal secret police force to crush protests, and let corruption in government go unchecked.

• To crack down on the growth of fundamentalist Islam, he allowed some reforms, such as giving the vote to women, and changing clerical land laws. These made fundamentalists oppose him even more.

• The influence of the USA, who had helped the shah re-take the reins of government from the elected prime minister in 1953, was deeply resented.

• Oil revenues were not used to develop the country, but simply made a few people very rich. Poor people increasingly turned to radical movements.

CONSEQUENCES

• A fundamentalist Islamic regime, withdrawing human rights, particularly women's rights, oppressing religious minorities, and applying Islamic law such as public executions and mutilations.

• The "hostage crisis", the seizure of 63 hostages at the US embassy (Nov 4, 1979–Jan 20, 1981) creates lasting enmity of the USA.

• International isolation as neighboring countries are fearful of Iran-sponsored Shi'ite rebellions.

Up to about 1978 most opposition to the shah came from the intellectual middle-classes, who wanted a liberal, constitutional government. But from 1978 radical Shi'ite Islamic clerics, particularly the Ayatollah (religious leader) Khomeini, inspired protests and mobilized students and the masses.

Main Centers of Anti-shah Demonstrations, 1978

TURKEY
Tabriz
CASPIAN SEA
TURKMENISTAN
SYRIA
Tehran
Qom
LEBANON
AFGHANISTAN
IRAQ
JORDAN
Yazd
ISRAEL
Abadon
IRAN
SAUDI ARABIA
PERSIAN GULF

KEY DATES

Jan 1978	Students in the city of Qom protest a libellous story about Khomeini in the official newspapers and are dispersed by the army; 70 students killed.
Feb–May	Memorial demonstrations are held; 100 demonstrators killed in Tabriz; attacks made on western buildings such as luxury hotels.
Sep	Martial law introduced. Demonstrations banned.
Sep 8	"Black Friday" – the army turns machine guns, tanks, and helicopters on demonstrators.
Dec 12	Two million people demonstrate in Tehran against the shah. The army refuses to fire on them. Sections of the army join protesters.
Jan 16, 1979	Shah leaves Iran.
Feb	There are two centers of authority: the remainder of the government, and Khomeini's Islamic Republican party.
Nov	After clashes with the Ayatollah, the secular prime minister, Mehdi Bazargan, resigns and the Islamic faction takes control. Ayatollah Khomeini becomes supreme leader.

KEY PERSONALITIES

Shah Mohammad Reza Pahlavi, 1919–80
Sep 16, 1941 Becomes shah after the Allies depose his German-sympathizing father during World War II. Remains close to USA and Britain. 1953 With help of CIA overthrows the prime minister. 1975 Makes Persia a single-party state. Oct 22, 1979 Visits USA, precipitating Iran hostage crisis. Dies in exile in Egypt.

Shapour (Shapur) Bakhtiar, 1915–91
1940s Fights for France against Nazi Germany. 1946 Takes up political career in Iran. 1953 Is deputy minister of labor in Mohammad Mosaddeq's government, which is overthrown by the shah. Imprisoned for illegal political activities, i.e. opposition to the shah. 1978 As a concession to protesters, chosen by the shah to lead a civilian government to replace military rule. Jan 1979 Persuades the shah to leave Iran. Tries to calm the country: dissolves secret police; calls Ayatollah Khomeini back from exile; promises free elections. Apr 1979 Leaves Iran after Ayatollah takes over. From France, leads opposition movement to Islamic republic. 1991 Assassinated by Iranians.

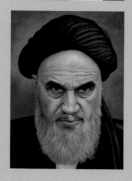

Ayatollah Ruhollah Musavi Khomeini, 1900–89
Born Ruhollah Mostafavi in Khomein. 1920s Becomes a Shi'ite cleric. 1963 Denounces shah's government, imprisoned, and narrowly escapes execution. 1964 Sent into exile. Calls for creation of theocratic state. His speeches, smuggled into Iran on cassette tapes, have widespread influence. Feb 1, 1979 Returns to Iran. Feb 11, 1979 Declares a provisional government, and takes power. Oversees creation of political system run by clergy. Bans Western cultural influences and calls for revolutions in other Arab states. 1980–88 Popularity increases when Iraq attacks.

The Balkans Conflict

The federation of Yugoslavia created after World War II was held together by President Tito. But the Yugoslavian republics and provinces were separated by ethnicity, religion, language, and historical hatred. Tito died in 1980, but the real death-knell for Yugoslavia was the collapse of communism in 1989. Power-hungry nationalists jumped into the political gap, and manipulated ordinary people into fighting each other.

A common sight in the Balkans Conflict: a young soldier patrols through a devastated city

CAUSES

Ethnic hatred Hatred between Serbs, Croats, Albanians, and Bosnian Muslims (Bosniaks) reached back for centuries. People were easily persuaded that they should have separate national areas.

Economics Slovenia and Croatia were the wealthiest regions of Yugoslavia. They did not see why their wealth should go to other areas, but the Serb-dominated rump of Yugoslavia did not want to lose these plum regions.

Territorial ambition Serbia and Croatia both tried to become larger by seizing parts of Bosnia (in full, Bosnia-Herzegovina).

CONSEQUENCES

- Yugoslavia fell apart, and Bosnia was divided in two.
- Ethnic hatreds were reinforced.
- Thousands of refugees could not or were afraid to return to their homes.
- An uncertain future for some areas, e.g. Kosovo, now a United Nations protectorate.
- The world was horrified by the revelation of rape camps as part of war and by the new phrase "ethnic cleansing".

Ethnic Divisions, 1991

Legend:
- Croats
- Serbs and Montenegrins
- Slovenes
- Muslims
- Macedonians
- Albanians

KEY FIGURES

Slobodan Milosevic, 1941–2006
Serbian politician. Considered main instigator of Bosnian war. **1987** Begins nationalist campaigns by claiming the provinces of Kosovo and Vojvodina. **1991** Proposes "Greater Serbia", encouraging Croatian and Bosnian Serbs to join him. **1995** Abandons Bosnian war after economic sanctions begin to hit. **2000** Voted out of office. **2002** Brought to The Hague to face war crimes trial. **2006** Dies of heart troubles in prison.

Franjo Tudjman, 1922–99
Croatian politician. **1939–45** During World War II fights for the multiethnic Partisan resistance. **1960s** Hailed as Croatian hero for his outspoken nationalism. **1989** Becomes leader of new Croatian nationalist party. **1990** Elected Croatian president, takes the lead in separatist movement. Introduces anti-Serbian laws. Provokes war in Croatia and spurs Bosnian Croats into fighting against Bosnian government.

Alija Izetbegovic, 1925–2003
Bosniak lawyer, politician. **1990** Wins Bosnian presidential elections. **Nov 1991** Anticipates trouble; asks for UN peacekeepers. Request refused. **1992** Tries to keep republic together as a multiethnic society, but refuses to capitulate to Serbs. **1996** Becomes president of the new, smaller Bosnia-Herzegovina federation. **2000** Leaves office.

KEY DATES

PRELUDE TO WAR

1990–91 In every republic, nationalists win the first free elections. Slovenia, Croatia, and Macedonia declare independence; Croatian Serbs vote to secede and join Serbia.

WAR IN SLOVENIA

Jul 1991 Serb-run Yugoslav army attacks Slovenia to keep it in the federation, but is forced to withdraw.

WAR IN CROATIA

Jul 1991 Serbian militias, helped by Yugoslav army, begin ethnic cleansing.

Jan 1992 Croats accept an internationally-brokered cease-fire; Serbs have won about a third of Croatia.

May–Aug 1995 Croat army attacks Serb-occupied Croatia and regains territories.

WAR IN BOSNIA

Mar 3, 1992 Bosnia declares independence; Bosnian Serbs declare they will join Serbia and are reinforced by Yugoslavian army.

Apr 6 Bosnian Serbs begin siege of Sarajevo and ethnic cleansing elsewhere.

Oct Bosnian Croats turn on Muslims.

Feb–Mar 1994 Croats agree a truce and federation with Bosniaks.

Jul 11, 1995 Serbs massacre c. 8,000 Bosniaks at UN safe haven Srebrenica.

Aug Serbs shell Sarajevo marketplace; NATO and UN react with real show of force.

Dec 14 Dayton peace agreement divides Bosnia into two: Muslim-Croat federation of 51% of Bosnia, Serb republic (49%), with the three ethnic groups sharing the presidency.

WAR IN KOSOVO

Feb 1996 Kosovo Liberation Army, representing oppressed Albanian majority, begins uprising against Serbia; Serbian response is condemned by international community as brutal and disproportionate.

Mar 1999 NATO bombs Serbia to stop Kosovo war.

Jun Kosovo handed over to UN/EU control but remains part of Serbia.

TROUBLE IN MACEDONIA

Feb–Sep 2001 Ethnic Albanians take arms against Macedonian majority but disarm on promise of greater rights.

MONTENEGRO

Jun 3, 2006 Montenegro splits from federation with Serbia.

The Bloodless Revolutionaries

Not every revolution has to be accompanied by violent uprisings. In some examples, the very sight of citizens gathering on the streets, peacefully expressing their displeasure with government, was enough to bring about a transfer of power to the people's choice. In others, a long period of non-violent protest was needed before changes occurred. While there were nearly always some deaths in these peaceful revolutions, the "bloodless" revolutionaries are those who tried to stop the violence, and who campaigned for change in peaceful ways. They include activists such as Nelson Mandela, who once embraced the need for armed uprising, but later rejected it.

Mahatma Gandhi lived a simple, spiritual life: he is seen here on his way to a meeting of the Indian National Congress in 1932, in the plain, traditional clothes he always wore

No power on earth could resist the lovers of liberty who were ready not to kill opponents, but be killed by them.
(Mahatma Gandhi, *Collected Works*)

MAJOR BLOODLESS REVOLUTIONS

1915–47	Gandhi's struggle for Indian independence from Britain.
Apr 25, 1974	Portuguese Revolution of the Flowers/Carnation Revolution/Armed Forces Movement. A military coup against a brutal 50-year-old dictatorship brings massive crowds out in support, offering red carnations to all soldiers. The regime falls.
Feb 22–25, 1986	Philippines EDSA Revolution. After disputed elections, at least a million people take to the streets to defend defectors from dictator Ferdinand Marcos' regime. They block the main road, Epifanio de los Santos Avenue (EDSA), and prevent troops moving in. Marcos flees abroad. The phrase "people's power" is coined to describe this revolution.
1989	Collapse of Soviet-run communism in east Europe. With USSR leader Mikhail Gorbachev indicating he will not interfere, first Poland then other east European communist countries throw off communism; Berlin Wall comes down, leading to re-unification of Germany; "Velvet Revolution" in Czechoslovakia.
1991	South Africa. Freed from prison, black rights leader Nelson Mandela renounces violence and negotiates peaceful end to apartheid in South Africa.
Jan 2001	Philippines EDSA II Revolution. A million people again take to the streets, especially EDSA, to protest against corruption under President Joseph Estrada. His government falls.
2003–05	Color Revolutions, east Europe. Waves of popular protests, all peaceful, triggered off by disputed elections, force the governments to resign in Georgia (Rose, 2003), Ukraine (Orange, 2004), Kyrgyzstan (Tulip, 2005).
2005	Cedar Revolution, Lebanon. Protesters force the downfall of Syrian-backed government and the withdrawal of Syrian troops.

BLOODLESS REVOLUTIONARIES

Mohandas Karamchand Gandhi, 1869–1948
Indian Hindu nationalist leader. Known as Mahatma, meaning "great soul". **1893–1915** Works as a lawyer in South Africa. **1896** Develops principles of non-violent, passive resistance to oppose laws discriminating against Indians. **1915** Returns to India to a hero's welcome; joins independence movement. **1921** Becomes leader of Indian National Congress; always stresses peaceful, non-cooperative protests but cannot prevent some violent outbreaks. Spends several periods in prison. **1930** Calls for new civil disobedience campaign, refusing to pay unjust taxes. Leads "salt march" from Ahmedabad 241 miles (388 km) to the sea to protest salt tax. **1932** Fasts to protest discriminatory treatment of low caste "Untouchables". **1947** India wins independence; fighting begins between Hindus and Muslims. **Jan 13–18, 1948** Fasts until bloodshed ends. **Jan 30, 1948** Assassinated by a Hindu fanatic.

Nelson Rolihlahla Mandela, 1918–
South African anti-apartheid activist, later president. **1942** Joins the African National Congress (ANC), campaigning for equal rights for blacks. **1948** Supports campaign of civil disobedience and non-cooperation through boycotts and strikes. **Dec 1956** Arrested for treason for contributing to Freedom Charter demanding basic rights. **Mar 29, 1961** Found not guilty, but forced into hiding by police harassment. Continues to campaign. **Jun 1961** Helps form military wing of ANC, prepared for armed struggle. **1962** Charged with sabotage after police find details of guerrilla training. **Oct 1962** Given life sentence at harsh Robben Island prison. **1984** Moved to less tough prison. **Feb 11, 1990** Released. **1991** Formally suspends armed struggle. **1993** Awarded joint Nobel Peace Prize with president F.W. de Klerk. Considered an "icon of reconciliation and forgiveness", and responsible for peaceful transfer to full democracy. **May 10, 1994** Inaugurated president of South Africa. **Jun 1999** Retires.

Mikhail Sergeyevich Gorbachev, 1931–
Soviet Russian politician. **1985** Appointed general secretary of the Communist Party, i.e. leader of the Soviet Union. Launches program of liberalization and reforms: *glasnost* (openness) and *perestroika* (restructuring) to make USSR more democratic and efficient. Begins arms limitation talks with US. **1988** Announces "Sinatra Doctrine" for east European satellite countries – they can do it "their way", i.e. USSR will not intervene. **1990** Receives Nobel Peace Prize for ending the Cold War. Becomes president of the new non-communist parliament. **1991** Begins to dissolve the Soviet Union by allowing independence to six Russian republics. **Dec 8, 1991** Forms loose economic federation of remaining republics, Commonwealth of Independent States.

Lech Walesa, 1943–
Polish shipyard electrician and labor unionist. **1978** Helps organize free non-communist unions. **Aug 1980** Leads Gdansk shipyard strike which inspires further strikes around Poland; wins right for independent unions. **Sep 1981** Elected chairman of new union, Solidarity. **Dec 1981** Interned by government, fearing Soviet armed intervention. Solidarity suspended. **Nov 1982** Released, secretly continues to organize Solidarity. **1983** Wins Nobel Peace Prize. **1988** Prime minister General Jaruzelski opens talks, legalizes Solidarity, and allows it to run some political candidates. **Jun 1989** Helps Solidarity win parliamentary seats. Inspires change in other European communist countries. **1990** Elected president of Poland.